Penguin Education

Penguin Education Specials
*General Editor:* Willem van der Eyken

**Spare the Child**
The Story of an Experimental Approved School
W. David Wills

W. David Wills studied social studies at Birmingham
University, and trained as a psychiatric social worker at the
New York School of Social Work. He has worked as head of
several experimental residential institutions for delinquent
or maladjusted children and young people: Hawkspur Camp,
Barns Hostel School for 'unbilletable evacuees', Bodenham
Manor School for maladjusted children, and Reynolds House
Hostel for maladjusted school leavers. He is now chairman
of the Homer Lane Trust, and of the governors of New
Barns School, Treasurer of the Planned Environment Theory
Trust and joint editor of *Therapeutic Education*.

He has published several books about his work including
*The Hawkspur Experiment* (1941, new edition 1967), *The
Barns Experiment* (1945), *Throw Away Thy Rod* (1960),
*Commonsense about Young Offenders* (1962) and *A Place Like
Home* (1970).

# Spare the Child
## The Story of an Experimental Approved School
W. David Wills

Penguin Books

Penguin Books Ltd, Harmondsworth,
Middlesex, England
Penguin Books Inc, 7110 Ambassador Road,
Baltimore, Md 21207, U.S.A.
Penguin Books Australia Ltd,
Ringwood, Victoria, Australia

First published 1971
Copyright © W. David Wills, 1971

Made and printed in Great Britain by
Hazell Watson & Viney Ltd,
Aylesbury, Bucks
Set in Linotype Pilgrim

# Contents

# Preface

This account of the experience of converting an orthodox approved school into a therapeutic community does not pretend to be an academic study and cannot even claim to be an unbiased history. Of what Richard Balbernie and his colleagues are doing I am an enthusiastic advocate, and this book is full of special pleading. It is because I am so deeply in sympathy with what is happening at the Cotswold Community that I have written the book, and only wish I had the skill to communicate my enthusiasm more effectively.

Even such as it is however I could not have written the book unaided and those to whom most thanks are due are of course those same people – Richard Balbernie and his colleagues. They are not only busy people, they are people with many preoccupations, but on my frequent prying visits they have managed to behave as if they had nothing better to do than to entertain me and to talk about what they were doing. Indeed I believe their own enthusiasm is such that they positively enjoyed doing so. I have failed if my admiration for them does not shine forth from almost every page I have written; my warmest thanks I offer them now.

The only one with whom I had any difficulty was Richard Balbernie himself. Him I saw from the beginning as what the novelists call the angle character, if not indeed as the hero of my story, but he objected to this and was constantly trying to get me to efface him. He gave me many hours of time, whether in talking face to face or in written communications; he provided me with masses of material of which I wish I had made better use; he was constantly solicitous about my physical well-being on my frequent overnight visits; he has read my manuscript (except this bit) several times at different stages, and his invaluable comments are almost as long as the book itself. But this awkward man has continually nagged at me to 'depersonalize' my story, to stop casting him in the heroic role, and to say more about what other people have done and suffered. Well, I see his point, and have tried to meet him as far as I can. But I cannot escape the fact that admirable as all those other people are, he was their leader. His was the vision, his the vocation and it was these qualities in their leader that evoked in his colleagues those virtues that I admire as much as he does.

Never did I imagine that the day would ever come when I would want to praise the Home Office, and now that it has I am too late, because the department I wish to praise no longer exists. The Children's Department (whose function has been taken over by the Department of Health and Social Security) bears no kind of responsibility for anything that appears between these covers, and will indeed disapprove of some of it. The efforts that they are making to create a new image for approved schools and to introduce a therapeutic approach to the treatment of young offenders are clearly beginning to bear fruit, and not by any means only at the Cotswold Community. For this I am very grateful because it is something I have longed to see. And as I know a little of the contrary pressures with which they have to contend I would like (if it is not an impertinence) to offer to them a word of praise, and one of encouragement to those who now take up their task.

I am grateful to my wife for many helpful suggestions as we went along; and to Christina Fox, who not only (for she is a musician) rescued me from the ignominious shame of writing *rallentando* when I clearly intended its opposite, but also — with a magnificent *accelerando* towards the end — made a fair copy of my execrable typescript.

# 1 The Children of the Perishing and Dangerous Classes

That was what Mary Carpenter called them 120 years ago. She had such a gift for the trenchant phrase that posterity remembers her more vividly than others of her day, and before it, who were concerned to do something constructive about the problem of wayward children. Nearly a century before Mary Carpenter, the Marine Society was formed 'for the purpose of clothing landsmen and boys for the use of the King's ships and as an expedient to provide for poor boys who might become a nuisance'!

Boys who might become a nuisance. A more temperate phrase than Mary Carpenter's, but one which recognized as early as 1756 a principle now entrenched in an Act of Parliament which has the effect of abolishing the schools which Mary Carpenter did so much towards establishing. The principle is that we need to concern ourselves not only with children who happen to have broken the law, but with all those whose circumstances are such that they 'might become a nuisance'. This was indeed the purpose of most of the early pioneers. The Philanthropic Society, for example, was not at first concerned with delinquent children so much as with destitute children who might become delinquent, and that is precisely the attitude of the new Act. The only difference is that the Act is concerned with emotional rather than economic destitution; it is poverty of the emotional life rather than lack of material things which brings about the state of mind leading to delinquent behaviour. We would not now consider a child delinquent who stole bread because he was starving, and the increase in crime of all kinds during the last prosperous quarter-century has led us all to review our ideas about the connection between poverty and crime. No longer are they the children of the perishing and dangerous classes;* they are, in the words of a recent Home Office document, 'Children in trouble'.

* *Reformatory Schools for the Children of the Perishing and Dangerous Classes and for Juvenile Offenders*, Mary Carpenter, 1851.

It was perhaps as 'perishing' rather than as 'dangerous' that Mary Carpenter and other early pioneers were most concerned with these children, but I think it is true to say that until recent years many of their successors seem to have been more concerned with the protection of society. Our new Act swings the pendulum again to concern for the individual child because, quite apart from any humane considerations, it is seen that only through loving concern for the individual child can the growth of a delinquent minority be prevented.

So far as we can tell, the schools which were established in the middle of the last century, following the efforts of such people as Shaftesbury, Adderley, Davenport Hill and Joseph Sturge, served a useful purpose for about a century. I say 'so far as we can tell' because reliable evidence about the degree of success they enjoyed is not easy to come by. In recent years, however, evidence has been more readily available, and it is not cheering. The criterion of 'success' (three years without a further conviction) is a crude one, but it has at least the virtue of objectivity, and the trend is unmistakable. In 1928 the reconviction rate was 21 per cent,* in 1962 it was 62 per cent,† and the decline was pretty steady over the years. Well may Julius Carlebach say ‡ that the system seemed to have become counter-productive. Few people would now talk of success and failure in these simple black-and-white terms, and the Home Office in its official reports has lately been careful to write 'success' in inverted commas; but in so far as the *aim* was in the past the crude one of discouraging further court appearances, success has certainly diminished over the last forty years.

Very differing views are put forward to account for this drastic deterioration, one of them being that the change is not so much in results as in the accuracy of the records, and I remember the late Margery Fry saying in private, when the 'success' figures were 70 per cent, that she wished she could believe it! Another theory is that as we have developed alternative methods of dealing with young offenders, only the more difficult type of child has reached the schools, which are thereby

*G. Rose, *Schools for Young Offenders*, Tavistock, 1967.
† *Report of the Work of the Children's Department*, 1964–6, HMSO.
‡ *Caring for Children in Trouble*, Routledge & Kegan Paul, 1970.

deprived of the leavening influence of the 'better' types. I believe that there has been a marked diminution in the success that has attended the efforts of the schools, but that this is due to changes that have taken place outside the schools, not to changes within them; that the schools have been unable to keep pace with the revolutionary changes that have taken place in society during the last half-century.

It is difficult as well as rash to make generalizations about some 120 schools dealing with about 8000 children whose ages range from 10 to 18 and whose intelligence varies as greatly as their ages. It must be borne in mind, moreover, that the schools are not part of a unified state system like prison and borstal; each one, though subject to Home Office Rules and to inspection by H.O. Inspectors, is a separate independent unit, about four-fifths of them run by voluntary bodies, the remainder by local authorities. Some of them take a more punitive attitude than others, some incline towards a therapeutic approach. In spite of all this, however, I believe it is possible to make certain very broad generalizations based on the history and traditions of the schools as a whole, and on the ethos of the society in which they came into being. They began, roughly speaking, with the Victorian era, during which the men and women who worked in them displayed an attitude which was directly derived from the society around them. When I say 'who worked in them' I mean precisely that and am not thinking of founders and committees, who may well have been, and often were, ahead of their time. But it is much easier to propound lofty principles on which a school is to be run, than it is to maintain those principles in the day-to-day life of the establishment. Mary Carpenter tried to do it herself as 'Lady Superintendent', but it was notable that she could never find anyone to maintain her standards during her frequent absences. This attitude of society with which the staffs of the schools were imbued was so impregnated with instinctive feelings, so charged with emotion, so rooted in Victorian theology and withal so deeply ingrained, that change was difficult; when to that is added the inertia that develops in all established institutions, change becomes almost impossible.

We see how necessary change became when we look at the characteristic feelings of our Victorian forbears about wayward young people. The motives of the founders of early reformatory schools were of the highest. They were Christian men and women who thought of themselves as rescuing perishing sinners, and there were certain basic assumptions that none of them would have dreamed of questioning. The first of these was that society was stratified for ever into castes and there was a tendency (unconscious rather than explicit) to assume a connection if not between riches and virtue, certainly between poverty and vice, though which caused the other was not clear. It was assumed that the aim of the schools was to produce obedient subservient members of the lower orders who would always be polite to their betters and be perfectly content with that station in life to which they had been allocated by divine providence and the school managers. While no doubt the pious founders thought of their employees as also belonging to the lower orders, *they* regarded themselves as representatives of the gentry, and demanded a suitable deference from the children in their charge. Say 'Sir' when you speak to me.

The next assumption was that misbehaviour was due to moral depravity, and while the growth of this was to be prevented so far as possible by removing the children from evil surroundings, and keeping them from the contaminating influence of prison, any actual evidence of it in the child's conduct must be punished. Punishment was thought of not merely as a device for enforcing acceptable behaviour; it was a divinely ordained consequence of evil, and the master who imposed the penalty was the representative not only of the gentry, but of the gentry's God.

It was further assumed that the standard of living in the schools – for the inmates, that is – must be very spartan indeed. The Poor Law with its doctrine of Less Eligibility laid down that the poor in the workhouse must not be as well fed and clothed as the poor outside it, and this doctrine applied *a fortiori* in the case of those who added depravity to poverty.*

These then were the basic assumptions of those responsible for schools in Victorian days and they reflected the general attitude of society in the middle of the nineteenth century. Yet

*See J. Carlebach, *Caring for Children in Trouble*.

there is perhaps a distinction to be drawn between the general public who held those views and the individuals who actually put them into practice. The position of the public hangman was somewhat analogous; even those who most ardently supported the death penalty as an instrument of social justice were apt to wonder what kind of man he could be who actually carried it out, and we are entitled to wonder what kind of man he was who carried out society's wishes about the young offender.

He was often a man of the highest Christian principles and the loftiest of motives, who derived great satisfaction from his work. It is not unreasonable to assume that the same man was often one in whom current theological ideas had induced deep guilt feelings, whose unconscious motive in entering this work was to expiate his own guilt vicariously in punishing others, and by the same means to subdue his own instinctive impulses to 'evil'. For better or for worse Victorian theology has gone, but there are still many people with guilt feelings to be assuaged. In very many cases too then, as now, he would be a man with a desire – however unconscious – to exercise power over others. This unconscious motivation was not, and is not, peculiar to people who work in approved schools. It is to be looked for and will often be found in any who feel strongly drawn to one of the professions which assume the duty of exercising authority over others, whether directly, like teachers or officers in the armed services or in prison, or indirectly, like social workers, parsons and doctors. Such men could derive enormous satisfaction from the imposition of severe discipline, and the expression of contempt or worse for the 'evildoer', but they would have no doubt whatsoever that what they were doing was for the good of the boys in their care. Of course this was not peculiar to the staffs of approved schools. In many public schools discipline was notoriously harsh within living memory, and one must believe that the same unconscious motives were at work there. Until about thirty or so years ago one frequently saw in *The Times* personal column advertisements inserted by country parsons and others, who were prepared to receive the difficult sons of middle- and upper-class parents for coaching and discipline – the sternness of the discipline was often strongly emphasized. But the fact that boys in approved schools were there because they were 'bad' made rationalization so much the easier for their masters, and the further fact that the approved schools dealt with large groups and the staff was by present standards small would make a measure of regimentation essential.

This general public attitude to the young offender meant that a type of man was attracted who derived satisfaction from its expression, and this would make change difficult; even when the public attitude became a little less primitive, men seeking such satisfactions would still look for them among those who have broken the law. Managers, as the years passed, might come to a more enlightened attitude and they might appoint a man who it was hoped would give expression to those views. But the fact remains that many of the men offering themselves for employment would be those seeking the kind of satisfaction I have referred to and who, once in their post, would hand down their ideas to the young men joining the service.

It is not to be thought for one moment that such men were anything but well intentioned. They were, and indeed are, usually men of the highest integrity who lacked, however, what is only now becoming to be seen as an essential qualification for such work – an awareness of their own unconscious motivation.

The schools then became, in the last century, disciplined hierarchies, and it is highly probable that so long as the boys who left them found themselves entering a society similarly structured, in which the lower orders had been brought up to be content with their station in life and touch their forelocks to their betters, only a small proportion committed further offences. But that is not the world of today. Society has changed out of recognition, but the schools, while they have changed, are still in many cases easily recognizable for what they were. They vary enormously, and some are making a real effort to escape from the old traditions and old ways of looking at things. But the tradition is so strong that escape is extremely difficult, and there are still schools in which there is an attitude that I can only describe as crypto-punitive. That is to say, while lip-service is paid to a different attitude, there is an underground current of feeling, seldom expressed or admitted, that the disciplined regimentation that is held to be necessary with large groups of boys is not only 'good for them', but is no more than they deserve. Others are making great and praiseworthy attempts to move over if not to a wholly therapeutic approach, at least to one that is more in keeping with modern ideas about child care. But always tradition drags like a brake.

While it has rarely had the appearance of wanting to change too much too suddenly, the Home Office has been a constant source of gentle pressure for change, but there has been a tendency on the part of the schools to resist this pressure, and one of the reasons for this resistance has undoubtedly been the fear of losing satisfaction of unconscious wishes. There has of course been a general loosening of discipline and a raising of material standards, but any enlightened headmaster who sought to make radical changes would find himself faced with strong resistance – not always conscious – from his staff, and if his principal opponents were unable to defeat him they would move to other schools that were more in keeping with their attitude. The result of all this has been that while some schools have changed fairly radically, change over the whole field has been limited. On the whole, while success rates have steadily declined, order and a superficial 'happiness' has been maintained in the schools, but from time to time tensions and pressures boiling below the surface have produced an outburst, such as the murder of a master at Standon Farm School in 1947, the Carlton outbreak in 1959, the Court Lees affair of 1967, as well as others which have not reached the newspapers.

One of the consequences of this hierarchical, crypto-punitive discipline was that it was liable to lead to a total lack of communication between staff and inmates, and it facilitated the growth of vicious subcultures among the boys. Anyone who has been in the ranks in any of the services is aware of the front that is presented to officers, and how it is often parodied by the person who has just been using it as soon as the officer's back is turned. The same kind of thing takes place in any highly disciplined organization (except perhaps a religious order; but who knows?), and as it does not seem to militate against the maintenance of that discipline no one worries about it, though individual officers may try to persuade themselves that *their* relationship with the men is different. When our concern is not merely the maintenance of discipline but the development in young people of a mature personality and a good character, it matters a great deal. A boy who presents a frank, compliant and pleasing façade to his superiors can acquire the reputation of being honest and cooperative while carrying on *sub rosa* all manner of enormities. I remember very well a senior leader in my house in borstal of whom we all thought very highly. It was not until he and I had both left borstal that I learned from another old borstalian that he was a leader in the subculture as well as in the formal discipline-culture, acting by means of his leader's privileges as a channel for illicit activities outside the institution, exacting tribute from younger boys, and not hesitating to use the official machinery of report and punishment as a weapon against any boy who dared to dispute his underground authority. Beatings-up were only used when the housemaster's punishments (for offences perhaps committed, but wholly irrelevant to the real reason they had been reported) were not deemed severe enough. This boy was every bit as vicious and criminal when he left borstal as when he entered it, but we of the staff never knew because there was no communication – no *real* communication – between us; we saw only the façade presented to authority. Between us there was an unbridged chasm across which we could see each other operating the machinery, and we on our side of the chasm thought it was the same machinery. It was as if the priest were celebrating Mass before the altar, and someone else the Black Mass behind it. The victims of this system have no redress because their 'masters' can use against them both the resources of the formal discipline, and the hidden terror of the subculture.

That was borstal and, be it said, it was thirty-five years ago. But it is a natural and inevitable outcome of any rigid system of disciplined castes in an enclosed community that a kind of parody of the system will develop underground, among those at the bottom of the hierarchy, whether it is prison, borstal, approved school, ordinary boarding school or children's home. The worst excesses of subculture tyranny can be avoided, and often are. They are avoided when the head is aware of the likelihood of the existence of a subculture and takes steps to see that those things that cause it – rigidity of castes, discipline for its own sake, a punitive or crypto-punitive outlook – do not exist in his institution. They are avoided when the head and his colleagues see discipline merely as a means of maintaining the necessary minimal order in a large group of people living together, and not as a means of training character or of giving young criminals a taste of what they deserve.

So long, however, as the institution is highly disciplined the danger of an illicit and vicious subculture exists, and if the staff are more interested in a quiet life than in helping their charges, it will flourish. The staff may well be, and usually are, totally unaware of its existence, and in the worst schools they not only take no steps to assure themselves of its non-existence but are even sometimes in collusion with it by the infliction of unofficial punishments. A staff member who strikes a boy outside the organized provision for corporal punishment is liable to instant dismissal, but the danger of dismissal in the kind of school I am thinking of is extremely remote because the whole ethos of the establishment is opposed to the laying bare of hidden sores.*

It may be thought that I am painting a very black picture of approved schools, and I should not like to be misunderstood about this. Many of them have done admirable work and have managed to avoid the worst of the evils of which I have been speaking. What I am concerned at the moment to stress is that the long-held tradition of the schools is a disciplinary, authoritarian, 'training' one; that this tradition lingers on because it satisfies unconscious needs in many of those who administer it; and until that tradition can be totally extirpated there will always be a grave danger of even the best schools relapsing into the evils of non-communication and delinquent subculture. Only a change of head may be needed to bring it about. The remedy is a totally different approach, one that may be described as a therapeutic approach, which sees the children basically as unhappy, deprived persons who need care and healing, and not as wicked children who need to be 'taught to behave'. For that is what they are – the casualties of society. We may be – and it is

*For an account, by an approved-school boy, of the subculture at work, see Steven Slater's *Approved-School Boy*, William Kember, 1969.

proper that we should be – horrified by some of the things they do; but we must never allow our horror of the things they do to blind us to the tragic circumstances which made them capable of doing things of which we think ourselves incapable. It may have been rash of me to generalize about approved schools, but I can safely generalize about their populations. They have all (up to now – the new Act, as we shall see later, changes this) arrived at the schools on the authority of an approved-school order made by a juvenile court. About seven-eighths of them have committed an offence which, if they had been adults, would have merited imprisonment, and about 90 per cent of these offences were against property; only 2 per cent were crimes of violence. Most of the other 8 per cent were sent to the schools because they were found to be in need of care, protection or control, or were in breach of a probation order. Whether or not they have committed a crime, however, the duty of the court is to take whatever action serves the best interest of the child concerned. And again, whether or not they have committed a crime, the vast majority of them will have acquired what can best be described as a delinquent orientation. That is to say, although very few have been deliberately en-couraged in delinquent behaviour by their parents, they will tend to have a measure of familiarity with delinquent ways, habits of thought and attitudes to society. This is not true of all who appear before the court, but it tends to be true of those whom the court sends to approved schools.

These are rough and broad generalizations, for I am not writ-ing a study of approved-school boys.* But the final and most important generalization I want to make is this : however hard and fierce the front they present to their peers, to the police, to the magistrates and to any set in authority over them, they are behind that brave front frightened, wounded, damaged, in-adequate little boys. If they seem to be – as they often are – without feeling for others, it is because they have experienced in the early years of their young lives so little feeling *from* others. A large proportion of them are neglected or rejected by one parent or the other – sometimes both. If we probe into the

*Fuller details of what kinds of boy reach approved schools will be found in G. Rose, *Schools for Young Offenders*.

background of the very worst of them we find that the serene and happy infancy, the tender solicitude of loving parents which made us the stable and upright persons we smugly believe ourselves to be, are something entirely unknown to them, an experience they never enjoyed. To subject such children to the rigours of the old type of approved school with its emphasis on discipline and obedience is to continue the deprivation they have already suffered and to perpetuate the defences they erect against it, bringing them to manhood still knowing nothing of tenderness, of compassion, of concern for others, still sheltering behind their protective covering of heartlessness and bravado.

The Home Office seems to have recognized the need for a total break with the past in the decision to incorporate approved schools in the existing system of provision for children needing care; this book is an account of the experience of one school which, anticipating future trends, set about converting an orthodox approved school into a therapeutic community. It is not the only one of its kind. Many other schools are taking a fresh look at their objectives, and looking for new paths towards them. Some have been doing so gradually and gently for years, some are making bigger changes more recently. It is not practicable to write about them all, so I have written about one. Perhaps it is the one that has made the most complete change the most suddenly; certainly it has experienced greater difficulties than most, partly because of the rapid and radical nature of the change, partly because of irrelevant problems by which the staff were beset when the inherent difficulties of the task were at their height.

The total transformation that has taken place, and is still taking place, and the troubles and perplexities encountered *en route* contain the elements of a story which is not only enthralling in itself but is one which, as it describes work that is being done in their name, the public should know about.

# 2 Ending the Old Way

In 1940 the Rainer Foundation, which is concerned with the care and treatment of delinquent children and young people, opened a new approved school, in the intermediate range; that is, for boys of thirteen or fourteen on admission. For this purpose it took over and adapted a property in Wiltshire, on the south-west edge of the Cotswolds, which formerly had been in the hands of a religious community, who had built premises to suit their own needs. The school soon acquired an excellent reputation, and the name of its first headmaster, C. A. Joyce, is well known. Early in the 1960s Mr Joyce took over other responsibilities in connection with the Rainer Foundation and gave up his work at the school.

Some seven years later the Foundation, which is a very forward-looking organization, decided after much thought and study that the time had come for radical change, and appointed Richard Balbernie to the headship, with the mission of converting Cotswold School into a therapeutic community to be known as the Cotswold Community.

When I heard this I was fascinated, for two reasons. The first is a very personal one. My own early ambition had been to work in approved schools, and I acquired what seemed to me to be suitable qualifications. Alas, those qualifications did not impress the people responsible for the schools, who at that time would appoint only teachers or skilled craftsmen. With youthful arrogance I scorned to acquire the training *they* considered appropriate (though to be sure additional training was not in those days easy to come by, for a penniless young man) so my ambition was never achieved. In any case I should have been quite unacceptable because my conception of the ideal approved school was an establishment whose methods were based on love and care rather than on discipline and training, where people strove to provide for the child's emotional needs from an informed knowledge of his problems. In fact, making due allowance for advances that have been made since those days in the understanding of young delinquents, I wanted to run what would in these days be called a therapeutic community. Hence then my excitement (for that is what it was) when I learned, as my retirement from professional work drew near, that such a community was to be founded in what hitherto had been an orthodox approved school.

My original ambition having been thwarted, I eventually found myself working with a similar* type of child who, having been caught up by a different bit of the administrative machinery, had been labelled maladjusted instead of delinquent. And here we come to the second reason for my interest in the Cotswold Community. In my work with maladjusted children I had met Richard Balbernie as a colleague. In 1951 he had started a boarding school for maladjusted children, Swalcliffe Park, of which I had heard nothing but good, but with which he had not been satisfied. In his book *Residential Work with Children* (published in 1966), Balbernie says in effect that at Swalcliffe he had come to realize that he had not the knowledge, the training or the skill even fully to understand the children's needs, much less to supply them. In 1955 therefore he handed the school over to someone else and went off to equip himself more thoroughly. His qualifications were already such as most people would have considered quite adequate, but by the time he came to the Cotswold Community in 1967 his academic qualifications consisted of a degree in psychology, training as a teacher, as an educational psychologist and as a psychotherapist, and a good deal of research work. His experience included work in all the various areas of his training, both with maladjusted children and with adults in an analytically orientated community. He wanted to equip himself to do a thorough professional job, but he had also a quality which enormously enhanced the value of his formal qualifications – he had what Quakers call a *concern* to help delinquent children. As long ago as his wartime

---

*Similar, not identical. The differences are rather in symptoms than in causes, and few people will nowadays dispute the fact that approved schools contain a large number of children who are both delinquent and maladjusted; nor that in such cases the delinquency is usually a symptom of the maladjustment.

service in the army he had decided that he must work with young delinquents, but he soon realized that if he was to make a real, professional, workmanlike job of it, he must examine and understand his motives (which his personal analysis helped him to do) in the hope that in any leadership role he undertook he would be able to act with clear, conscious understanding of exactly what he was doing.

Although this book is about the Cotswold Community and not its principal, it is clear that what such an institution *is* depends in large measure upon the quality of the man who is leading it. But now I heard something else which increased my interest. Balbernie, I was told, was expecting to carry out this transformation with the existing staff. Now that, I thought, is surely impossible, and was certainly something I would never have attempted myself even if I had been given the opportunity. There will be men, I argued (rightly as it transpired), who have been there for ten, fifteen, twenty years or more, who have faithfully and loyally served the school under the old dispens-ation, and who cannot fail to regard the new approach as an implied condemnation of all that had gone before. However diplomatic, however tactful, however persuasive the new man is, he will be saying in effect, 'Your faithful service through all these years has been faithfulness to a mistaken ideal; your loyalty over all these years has been a misplaced loyalty.' I did not see how the staff could see it otherwise, nor how a man could possibly accept the 'fact' that what had been done all these years was 'wrong', especially when the man who app-roached them in this way came from outside the approved-school service. Furthermore, although I did not realize this until later, these same men would have served under Mr Joyce, and although seven years had passed since then they looked back to those days with deep nostalgia as the golden age, and longed for someone who would provide the same kind of charismatic leadership, bringing back the glories of the golden age in detail. Resistance would be strong and so emotionally charged that Balbernie must be annihilated by the forces that would be arraigned against him. I did not see how he could possibly survive. It is true that, although we had met from time to time over the years, I did not know Balbernie well, but I did not see how *any* man could survive in such circumstances. I confess that this last fact gave a rather ghoulish quality to my interest, and when about a year after the changeover I was given an opportunity to visit the Community, I took it.

I was simply astonished by what I found there. Physically the place was a shambles. At the heart were some pleasant enough buildings in the local stone and roughly the local tradition, arranged round two quadrangles, faintly reminiscent of an Oxford college. But outside these squares around the whole periphery, in the flat Wiltshire land among the worked-out gravel beds, was a desolation of cheap one-storey concrete buildings, some decaying, some decrepit, and among them a couple of modern buildings – equally cheap – in glass and weatherboard. Concrete roads and paths, leading apparently to nowhere except desolate derelict buildings, heaps of rubble, and metal debris lying about here and there. In the midst of this wilderness I found Balbernie. I do not suggest that he was entirely unshaken by the experience he had undergone, though that experience, as I shall show, was quite as shattering as I had imagined; but he had survived. He had survived, moreover, with his sensitivity and his integrity untouched. 'Oh yes,' said one of his senior colleagues when I was expressing my admiration recently, 'Richard's got what it takes. That MC wasn't one of the kind that comes up with the rations.'

When Balbernie arrived at the Cotswold School in the autumn of 1967 he knew in general terms exactly what he wanted to do, though he had only the vaguest idea how in the particular circumstances it was to be done. One of his aims could be described as the establishment of a community of stable, concerned adults and delinquent children, where communication was uninhibited by artificial barriers, so that some of the qualities of the adults could 'rub off' on to the children. That is a very crude way of putting it. He knew that a major problem of the delinquent boy who has been committed to an approved school is that at a vital time in his life, when he was beginning to look forward to manhood, he had lacked adequate models of what constitutes a good, masculine man. This may have been because he had no father, or no effective father in the sense that he did not concern himself with his family but spent all his even-

ings in the 'local'; or the father himself was immature or delinquent or both, or the mother despised her husband, or the
relationship between father and son was so unsatisfactory that
the boy turned away from everything his father stood for – including authority, which of course includes teachers and other
possible adult models. Instead he would take for his standard
equally immature and undeveloped young people of his own age
group, and thus become stuck with primitive concepts of masculinity. In consequence of this, the masculine strength and the
perfectly proper masculine aggression he was beginning to acquire, he learned how to use only in primitive destructive ways,
in domination, in violence, in automatic unreasoning opposition
to all authority. Even those who had not the physique or the
courage to express themselves in this way would still hold it
before themselves as the masculine ideal, and would perhaps be
unhappy because they could not live up to it. They would
become the hangers-on, the 'toadies', the admirers of the delinquent gang-leaders, and more often than not the ones who would
be caught when as a group they engaged in delinquent activities.

It was necessary therefore to put before these boys good
models of masculinity, men who were strong and reliable, and
took pleasure in doing a good day's work; men who were concerned for others and, so far from using their strength to harm,
were not ashamed to use 'Man's strength to comfort man's
distress'. They had to be men, moreover, of authority who knew
and were able to show that authority is not something that
depends upon a system of controls handed down through an
hierarchy, but something within a man; something that arises
from his own integrity and confidence in himself, and which
makes those around him feel safe.

Cotswold School, like most approved schools, was a place
where it was difficult to display that kind of authority. All
authority, all responsibility, was vested in one man, the headmaster, who was at the top of a chain of command, so that staff
were in a sense prevented from exercising authority in their
own person. They were acting, in whatever they did, on behalf
of the head, and any boy who proved difficult was passed up
the command-ladder to a point consonant with the enormity of
his offence, ending with the headmaster who alone could beat

or expel. This fact – that little real authority was vested in anyone but the head – would tend to arouse in the minds of the boys a measure of contempt for less senior staff, and this alone would tend to make them inadequate models. On the other hand the regimentation,* the shouting of orders, the exercise of authority based on a system of punishments with corporal punishment as the final resort, accords very well with the immature conception of masculinity so far acquired by the boys and gives them in effect a licence to behave similarly themselves. Some may object to my reference to a system of punishments on the grounds that it was a system of *rewards* and punishments. But as the 'rewards' consisted merely of the tardy return in the guise of 'privileges' of basic human rights such as freedom of movement and communication, I think my description is the proper one.

It was presently discovered that the boys had indeed constructed a kind of parody or caricature of the formal system of discipline, based entirely on the tyranny of a few boys. A thriving and vicious subculture permeated the school, which was so widespread in its incidence and so pernicious in its application that when its grim existence was revealed most of the staff simply refused to believe it. How long it had been in existence is not clear, but certainly for a period of years. There were 'governors' or 'deans' or 'daddies' in each of the four houses, who supervised cruel initiation ceremonies. There were beatings-up which began with a duffle-coat being thrown over the head of the victim so that he could not identify his persecutors. Boys had their hands tied to a hot water pipe just at the point that it left the boiler; boys were made to masturbate themselves or each other for the amusement of the bullies; there was a system of homosexual prostitutes; and of course helotry was widespread. The protection rackets were a precise parody of

* In one house 'Some thirty boys were made to clean their teeth in unison, in lines where toothbrushes were taken out, everybody put the toothpaste on together, everyone brushed each jaw regularly so many times. They all turned and spat together and then they took water in their mouths and they all swilled their mouths together and they all spat together again.' (From a private paper written by a staff member, and used for staff discussion in the early days of the change.)

the official system of 'rewards'. All ownership of property, all comfort and ease, all safety and dignity were rudely swept away from the generality of boys by the bullies; but if you were complaisant, and toadied, and allowed your body to be used at the whim of the 'dean' and his friends, then some of it might, as a special favour, be returned to you for just so long as you toed the line. But once step out of line and you not only lost it all, but were brutally punished into the bargain.

About this terrible regime there was among the boys a profound conspiracy of utter silence. Those who suffered under it (and every boy suffered under it when he first arrived) were called suckers, and the domination of the bullies was so complete, so absolute, that its victims were too terrorized even to contemplate the further suffering to which they would be subjected if they dared to 'grass'. Or perhaps it is incorrect to refer to it as a conspiracy of silence. It may not be too fanciful to suggest that they did not conspire to keep these things out of sight any more than an individual person deliberately determines to keep out of sight those parts of the human psyche that we call unconscious. These things are called unconscious because we are in a real sense unconscious of them; we do not even know that we have repressed them. So with the subculture that often exists under hierarchical discipline – it may be thought of as the community's unconscious, and although like all analogies it is undesirable to carry it too far, this could well be the reason that it is quite possible to assert with complete sincerity 'These things do not exist'. Many indeed will claim that they do not and did not exist, here or elsewhere; and my reference to them at the Cotswold is not in censure or criticism of any individual person. I have felt it right to refer to these conditions because of my strong conviction that they are liable to arise wherever men are expected to operate a system of disciplined, authoritarian control over delinquent boys, however excellent and admirable those men may be. It is in my view inherent in the system, and I doubt whether it can be totally eradicated so long as the system exists. I believe little blame if any attaches to managers or inspectors who fail to uncover such evils, because they are so deeply embedded, hidden and entrenched that they are undiscoverable from outside, and virtually undiscoverable from within. The only way to make sure they do not exist is to see to it that such establishments become true communities of young people and adults (as distinct from disciplined hierarchies), where the chief concern of the adults is therapeutic care, exercising control only through true affective relationships. This kind of regime the Rainer Foundation was determined to establish, and this clearly is the kind of purpose which animates the new approach to residential treatment embodied in the Children and Young Persons Act of 1969.

If any blame attaches to anyone, it attaches to all of us, and this is why I think it right to make public what I have written above. We are all delinquents beneath the skin in the sense that we have instinctive desires and impulses which if left unchecked would lead to anti-social and even violent behaviour. But though we do keep them in check, we are still afraid they might one day erupt in us, we are even a little jealous of those in whom they do erupt, as well as being frightened of them. For this reason we all tend to want to react with some violence when we see them emerging in others – we want to make the guilty party a scapegoat for our own guilt, our own delinquent tendencies. This is why penal reformers found it so extremely difficult to secure the abolition of birching and flogging; there was ample and irrefutable evidence that they served no useful purpose in relation to those upon whom they were inflicted, but they did serve another purpose – they allayed our collective sense of guilt, our collective fears about our own unconscious urges. From this source – the unconscious desire for a scapegoat – there is constant pressure upon all those who deal with offenders to be more and more punitive, to punish us all – but vicariously.

Unless those who work in approved schools and similar places are perfectly clear about their precise task, they are almost bound to succumb to the pressures thus placed upon them. There *has* been uncertainty in the past about the role of approved schools. They have – as I suggested in the previous chapter – a punitive tradition from which the scapegoating pressures of society make it difficult for them to escape, and they have been uncertain in the extreme whether their function was one of disciplined training or therapeutic care. They have in recent years tried to do both, but the two approaches are not miscible. In these circumstances of uncertainty the pressure of society tends always to push in the direction of discipline and punishment, and wherever there is such an element in the attitude of the adults, it will create a crude and magnified reflection among the children with whom they work.

We are all to blame. But at least our elected representatives and our public servants are determined to see that the unhappy children who, by reason of emotional disturbance, faulty upbringing or from any other cause come into residential care, shall not in the future become the scapegoats of our inner guilt.

All these allegations about the existence of a cruel subculture at the Cotswold had begun to be made in great secrecy during the months preceding the change, and the loosening of the regime brought them forward in greater number. Whether or not the state of affairs that existed among the boys was due to the system under which the school was organized (and there can be more than one view about this; it was after all the system used in most approved schools) it is certainly true that these immature boys with their primitive conception of masculinity were ripe for corruption. And the subculture was – as such a thing always is – a distorted and corrupting reflection of the formal system of regimented discipline. In such a system the staff are a separate privileged caste, and the bullies of the subculture aped this by creating for themselves a similar separation and status, below ground. To the boys it could well seem that the main function of the staff was to keep them in subjection on behalf of the head – and this was what the bullies did for the 'deans' of the subculture.

This was the degree to which the boys had misused their male strength and drive for their mutual corruption, and Balbernie was able to survive the first terrible year partly at least because he was sustained by anger on the one hand and pity on the other. His task was to convert the subculture and this corrupt and corrupting atmosphere into a healing one, and while he could not see at once in detail how this transformation was to be brought about, certain things were very clear from the beginning. One was that he must make his position clearly understood right away. By pure ill-luck he had entered on his task at a time when there was already a good deal of turmoil in the place, to which two factors had contributed. One was the departure of his popular predecessor some months previously, and the other was the subculture revelations, which were greatly resented by some of the staff, who denied its existence or claimed that the allegations were greatly exaggerated. It seemed to him that he might as well pitch in and add his turmoil to the rest. Clearly the underground evils that had been revealed must be swept away and swept away quickly. No compassionate person of integrity could possibly live with them once they were revealed. (One may argue indeed that it was the very compassion and integrity of some of the staff – men who lacked Balbernie's psychological training and understanding – that made it impossible for them at first to accept the truth of the allegations.) Even if they were not necessarily inherent in the situation, they were much more likely to flourish under an imposed authoritarian discipline than in the kind of regime it was hoped to introduce. To that end therefore it seemed expedient to introduce the reforms immediately and forcibly. There was also present in Balbernie's mind the very real fear that in view of the turmoil already existing, if he tried to go slowly the pressures against change might be so strong that, over a long period, he might find them irresistible, and have to give up.

By rushing at it in the precipitate way he deliberately did, he was undoubtedly making an enormous amount of trouble for himself, but he considered all that and decided that it was not only the best, but the only thing to do. Other people have attempted and are attempting to introduce a therapeutic attitude into orthodox approved schools, but they have not had the misfortune to find themselves beset by such a number of other, irrelevant problems. They have therefore been able to move slowly and gently, educating their colleagues in the new approach as they went along, making each successive change after the last one had been accepted, gradually persuading the less responsive among the staff to seek employment elsewhere. I mention all this because I do not want it to be thought that the enormous problems that had to be faced at the Cotswold are necessarily to be faced, to such a degree, every time such a change is sought. It just happens that at the Cotswold at that moment there were these difficulties that seemed to make the bull-at-a-gate approach the only one feasible, and that, therefore, was the one Balbernie used.

The boys – a hundred or so – (and there had been many more than this in earlier days) lived in four houses, three of which formed the sides of the back square or quad, the front square being formed of staff houses and offices. In front of these houses every morning the boys were paraded and marched off to assembly in a hall outside the square. There they stood in rows with the staff round the sides in due pecking order. On the word of command all came to attention and in walked the head, who announced the hymn, uttered prayers and made announcements. Then they were all marched off again. To this assembly Balbernie was introduced on his first morning. He does not clearly recall how he got through this performance, nor what was said or done, but he straightway resolved that it would not do. The next day he had them arranged in a circle round the room, but after a few days dropped this fruitless relic of the past altogether.

So the change began. Simultaneously he made it clear to his deputy that whatever else might happen in the future, one thing they could start – or more properly end – immediately. There would be no more beatings. Corporal punishment was out. There had been beatings in the past at the rate of three or four a month for stealing, for absconding, for various offences against discipline, for sexual misconduct when it became so flagrant that no one could fail to be aware of it. The last two entries in the punishment book concerned attempted sodomy and attempted intercourse with a sow. They were in September 1967, since when there have been no entries at all.

The next thing to go was the grading system. A few days after Balbernie's arrival the deputy announced that a routine grading conference was due. Grading was the heart and soul of the system, as it was indeed in many if not most approved schools. It varied in detail from school to school, but it was the same in essence. If a boy toed the line, presented a pleasant demeanour to the staff, avoided being detected in any misbehaviour, worked hard and generally succeeded in creating what we used to call in borstal (where the same system operated) a 'good impression', he would be moved every two or three months into a higher grade until he reached the top one, which made him eligible not indeed for discharge, but for consideration for discharge. The effect of the approved-school order was roughly that a boy would be kept in the school for up to three years, and the boys commonly thought of it as a three-year sentence ('Three years for nicking a bloody bottle of milk off a doorstep'), which could be reduced by good behaviour. Grading was closely associated with length of 'sentence', because the more quickly a boy travelled up through the grades, the sooner he got out. But each grade carried with it certain 'privileges' which provided an added incentive to good behaviour – such things as exeats, home leave, pocket money and so on depended in large measure upon the grade a boy was in.

There were eight grades at Cotswold, but new boys began in grade three. Grades one and two were in effect punitive grades, for a boy could go down as well as up, and down grading was the common punishment for misbehaviour. It was necessary to have some punishment in reserve for new boys, so they started in grade three. Mild misconduct led to delay in upgrading, while serious misconduct led to downgrading. Snakes and ladders, Balbernie called it. As a system of control it may have had something to recommend it. As character training its value was dubious, and as therapy it was useless. It was based on the wholly fallacious assumption that a boy who was by its means coerced into conformity with the rules of the school, would on discharge obey the rules of society. I know of no grounds for such an assumption.

The grading conference consisted of the senior officers of the school and met in the boardroom. Here Balbernie found to his incredulous horror that they proposed to consider no fewer than ninety-two boys in the space of an hour or so. He went blindly through the motions that were expected of him ('All I could think of was EGGS'), put his initials in the book in the places where it was required, and resolved that this should be the last grading conference. And so it was. Not only were there no more grading conferences; there would be, he announced, no more grading. The grading system was done away with. It provided more than the wrong motive for behaviour; it provided also a kind of pattern to be parodied in the subculture, which had its own informal grading system with 'governors' and bullies at the top, new boys at the bottom, and in between them the mass of aspirants to the grade of governor or bully.

Perhaps the worst thing about it was its effect upon the emotionally disturbed boys who constitute a fair proportion of the population of any approved school. A boy who was not very maladjusted could watch his step, toe the line or at least see that his misdemeanours were not detected, thereby moving quickly up the grades – and out. Balbernie had made a five-year study of boys passing through another approved school, and had learned that the emotionally disturbed boys, and especially any of them who regressed (that is, reverted to an earlier and more infantile mode of behaviour – often an important preliminary to progress), were repeatedly downgraded and could only cope with the final stages of their 'indeterminate sentence' by repressing their problems, thus becoming deeply depressed. Such children 'could only get through the system by becoming temporarily submissive zombies'.

The abolition of grading had as a corollary another important change. Date of discharge hinged upon grading; how was that important matter to be arranged in future? Here a decision was taken which some may question, and which many certainly did question at the time. This said, in effect, 'We shall do away with what amounts to an indeterminate sentence. Every boy who comes here in future on an approved-school order will be told exactly how long he will be here. As the average length of stay in the past has been about eighteen months, that will be the actual length of stay for everybody from now on, neither more nor less. This will put one cause for anxiety right out of the boys' minds and it will cut at the roots of the tradition that an approved school is a place to get out of at all costs at the earliest possible moment. It also means that we can plan an overall treatment programme based on eighteen months.'

Whether this action was strictly in keeping with the law and the approved-school rules is far from clear, but the Home Office seem to have said nothing. They knew, as Balbernie and his committee knew, that the approved-school order was on its way out, and when the new Bill was passed boys would no longer be given a 'three years approved-school sentence'. That bill became law as the Children and Young Persons Act 1969, and by the time boys begin to arrive under the new arrangements laid down in that Act, the kind of regime will have been established in which the boy himself will be consulted about, and cooperate in, his treatment, in which it will be possible for him to remain at the school as long as he feels he needs it. It will then be no longer necessary to tell a boy he is there for eighteen months. The length of his stay will be something in which the boy himself is involved in a real and not an artificial sense.

In this context it is perhaps useful to recall that certain events outside the Community were bound to lead to some uncertainty and perhaps confusion within it. Hitherto the school had had no discretion concerning whom it received – they just had to take whoever was sent to them – but it had enjoyed complete discretion (within the regulations) concerning whom it discharged, and when. But now, as community homes, approved schools were to move into a new role under the new Act. The Cotswold Community at least (so long as it remained under the control of a voluntary body) would be able to make its own decisions concerning intake based on their evaluation of the boys' needs, and their ability to meet those needs, because eventually boys would come to them not on an approved-school order made by the court, but on the application of a children's officer after the court had made a care order. This was satisfactory, but it was not clear that the position concerning discharge was equally so. Much would depend upon the attitude of children's officers, and what that attitude was to be remained to be seen. To Balbernie – as presumably to any head of a community home – it was clear that a boy's removal from the community must hinge entirely upon task completion – he should move on when healing had gone as far as the community was able to take it. But the *authority* for his removal appears under the new Act to rest with the children's officer to whose care he has been committed; and supposing he takes an attitude of 'The Lord giveth, the Lord taketh away'? In such a case children could be arbitrarily removed from the Community before the task was completed, and there would apparently be no redress either for the child or for the Community. On the other hand, boys so committed to the care of the Children's Department would presumably, as now, under the Fit-Person Order, be in care until their eighteenth birthday. Would child-care officers, having found a good berth for a difficult boy at the Cotswold Community, want to leave him there until he passed out of care, rather than involve themselves in the wearisome task of finding another placement for him when the Community's job was done? This was one of the many external factors (and we shall hear of others) which were added to the internal anxieties with which the new management was beset, and its solution is still unclear.

To return, however, to those pressing internal anxieties. Within a very short time, as we have seen, the new head (who further dissociated himself from the past by calling himself principal) had switched off the engine that had made the school tick over, had hacked away all the previous bases of authority and order. The boys were as lost and alarmed as the staff. The staff did not see how order could any longer be maintained and the boys were deprived of a familiar way of life which, whatever its failings, did provide them with some kind of security. They knew where they were with it; they were lost without it. It is probable too that the leaders of the hidden subculture vaguely apprehended that their 'system' was likely to topple now that the system which it parodied was no longer there, and this apprehension affected not only the leaders. With a terrible ambivalence the unhappy, terrorized 'suckers' loved what they hated – 'they were crying out for punishment and needed it like some kind of breast'. The whole school seethed with resentment and hostility, all of it directed at one man, the principal. In facing all this venom, this hatred, he knew that he had the full support of the Rainer Foundation. They were solidly and indeed enthusiastically behind him. But they were far away, and within the Community itself there were at this time only two or three at the most among his fifty or so colleagues whom he knew he could regard as allies. Anyone who has lived with his family in a Community of this kind knows how hostility to a man can be reflected – often with exaggeration – among wives and families, and I need not dwell on the distressing side of this picture. Balbernie's downfall within weeks was being confidently predicted.

The measures so far taken – the abolition of corporal punishment, of the grading system, and of the 'indeterminate sentence' – were purely negative. It was necessary now to explain to the staff and to the boys what positive measures were proposed to replace them. Until those new measures began to take effect, no more new boys were to be taken. A series of staff meetings now began at which the principal tried to explain what was meant by a therapeutic community, a healing community, and especially – at this juncture – how this affected staff attitudes.

This, clearly, was not going to be easy. In the steps so far taken the staff had seen something of what kind of change was anticipated, and up to now it did not make sense to them. To many, if not to most, the new head was just a self-deluded 'softie'. They may have told themselves that he did not look like a softie, and his military record was not that of a softie, but it was very difficult for them to listen to him with patience. He had knocked away all the props, but he still expected the house to stand. What they had not yet grasped was that it was going to be rebuilt in a new way in which the stresses were so integrated into the structure that it was supported by its own weight and needed none of the buttresses with which they were familiar.

That they would be hostile Balbernie expected, and he was more or less ready for it, though perhaps not for the intense degree of animosity which was now displayed. It had always been obvious that men – many of them middle aged, some nearing retirement – who had spent most of their working lives operating the old system, and relying on that system, would quite reasonably see total loss of control as the immediate consequence now to be expected. It was also obvious that *some* of them would collude with, or even actively encourage, that disorder by standing back and saying, 'What can we do? He has taken our authority from us. Whatever happens now is his fault not ours', and that was what a few men did. It was difficult for them to see that what he was trying to do was not to take away their authority but to get them to accept and use real personal authority instead of relying on a system; but this is something not easily understood by men brought up in that system, nor could he be sure that all of them had the necessary personal integrity and self-discipline to be able to do it. One thing, however, compelled them at least to make the effort, and tended to prevent excessive collusion with disorder. It was made absolutely clear that one of two things was going to happen. The Cotswold School was going to change, or it was going to close. There was no further existence for the school as it had been. If the present attempt to change it failed, then it would close and they would all be out of a job. If they wanted to avoid that, then they must cooperate in the efforts now being made to bring about the change which alone could prevent it. This made sense, if the other did not. It was harsh, it was coercive, it was quite out of keeping with the kind of motives Balbernie hoped would ultimately animate the staff, and the kind of relationship he hoped to have with them. But for the moment it saved the day and prevented utter chaos.

It did not serve to make him any more popular, and the need to adopt such an attitude caused him some personal distress. Although there was much hostility – perhaps more hidden and oblique than overt – there was also, especially among the older men who had served under Mr Joyce, a feeling not so much of hostility as of perplexity – a kind of wounded perplexity. These were staunch, loyal men of integrity and real good-will. They hoped, as I have said, that the golden age of Mr Joyce was about to return, and were willing, even eager, to accept a charismatic, authoritarian leadership. A certain kind of authority they certainly did get, and quite unequivocally – an authority that said in no uncertain tones, 'Thou shalt not', and they were more than ready to accept its positive counterpart in 'Thou shalt'. But the kind of regime it was now hoped to establish, which pushed authority and responsibility on to the individual man, which called for a whole, totally different and special kind of attitude, was not one that was susceptible to direction from above in crisp orders and instructions. It involved a long slow process of learning – learning new ideas, a new approach, a new way of looking at things – and until all this had been learned there was, among even the best of these admirable men, perplexity and distress. To 'refuse' them the clear direction they sought was a form of unkindness that Balbernie hated, but he saw no alternative.

Added to all this perplexity there was much apprehension and perhaps some confusion and uncertainty arising from the backlash of the Court Lees affair,* which was still very much in the public consciousness and *a fortiori* in the consciousness of approved-school staffs. Public statements were being made by all and sundry in newspapers and journals about the need for change; this did nothing to enhance security and tranquillity. These statements were naturally read with interest and some foreboding by the Cotswold staff.

Events within and without the Community had thus combined to create in the staff a sense of precarious anxiety, and it was natural for them to look to their new head for clear and authoritative guidance out of their turmoil. It is not surprising that his 'failure' to provide this should evoke at the least uncomprehending resentment, and at most indignant hostility. Instead of a solution he presented them with a problem – the problem of learning a new approach to a job they felt themselves to have been doing competently for many years. And why, they tended to ask themselves, bother to do any such thing? For it must be realized that they had enjoyed very little contact with other workers in the field, were out of touch with developments elsewhere, and for the most part assumed that the ideas now being placed before them were entirely Balbernie's brain-children. It was to help them enormously when, a little later, they were to meet other people, people of authority and reputation, who shared this new outlook; but that was not yet, and there was naturally a strong tendency to write off the new man as a crank, and to resent such a person being placed in authority over them.

In these early talks with the staff it was essential to instil in them an understanding of one principle that is absolutely central to the idea of a therapeutic community. That title itself puts aside all thought of quasi-punitive discipline and training and substitutes the idea of healing; what we are concerned with

*Court Lees was an approved school which the Home Secretary had closed following allegations of excessive corporal punishment.

now is something that is at the heart of the therapeutic approach, and is concerned with human relationships. It is an
extremely difficult idea to put across. This is not because it is
new, but because it is familiar; not because it is difficult to
accept, but because everyone accepts it. We all know 'about' it,
even if we do not actually know it. It is basic to democracy,
and ours is a democratic society; it is integral in Christianity,
and our society has its roots in the Christian ethic. Every parson
and every politician preaches it, every teacher has it impressed
upon him in the course of his training. Everyone is familiar
with it, no one would dream of denying its truth; yet the only
people who are likely to admit that they do not practise it are
the few who really understand it.

There are many ways of expressing it, yet it is incredibly
difficult to put into words which completely comprehend its
full significance. It is expressed in many catch-phrases and
clichés that have become so commonplace and habitual that all
meaning has been eroded from them. We talk of respect for the
individual, the essential worth of human personality, human
dignity, the rights of man, the brotherhood of man, that of God
in every man, and so on and so on. The idea is expressed in a
thousand ways, but practised rarely.

It involves the ability never to lose sight of the potentialities
of any man, and to respect him for them. It means never des-
pising a man just because he seems to have failed to live up to
those potentialities. It means never being contemptuous towards
someone merely because he is younger or smaller or weaker or
stupider – or wickeder than us; it means not merely the end of
hectoring and bullying, not merely the end of patronizing and
condescending – these are its negative aspects; it means the
reverse of these things, in real, *felt* respect in everyday contacts
with other people. It means, for approved-school staff, listening
with interest and attention to what a boy has to say, and so
conducting oneself in one's attitude to him that he feels free to
say it. More than this, it means accepting what he has to say,
discussing it with him on frank and equal terms and, where the
occasion calls for it, taking action on the basis of that discussion.
It means an end to the age-old assumption that an adult may be
as abusive as he likes to a child, but the child may never abuse

an adult; the approach is one that takes away the occasion for the child's abuse rather than forbidding or punishing it. It is an approach which can only arise from an attitude of true humility and concern, and this is something which – if absent – does not grow overnight, nor to order. It involves a man's whole philosophy of life, and there are many – in the approved-school service and out of it – to whose philosophy of life it is wholly alien and repugnant, soil in which this plant can never grow.

Balbernie hoped there might be some among the staff to whom this new approach was not wholly inimical, who had hitherto swum with the tide because it was so overwhelmingly strong, and they had been unaware of the possibility of other currents. Them – if any should emerge – he hoped to encourage. For the rest, if he could not induce a change of heart, he could at least lay down certain prohibitions. Whether or not, he said in effect, you are able to show real respect and concern for these boys, at least you will not treat them with contempt. There will be no more numbering. No boy joining this school from this day forward will be given any number of any kind for any purpose. The use of unadorned surnames was henceforward absolutely forbidden. And there was to be no more, 'You boy! Come here.' Boys were to be known and addressed by their Christian names. This was an order. But there was a more subtle expression of the caste system and the devaluation of the boys to which he also put an end by order. It was common for the boys to use prison *argot*, talking of screws, rakeouts, deans, snout and so on, thereby associating themselves with a cut-off, exclusive, anti-social culture which in itself militates against therapy, but which can hardly be prevented by executive action. What *could* be prevented however was staff colluding with this damaging identification with the criminal ethos, by themselves using the same language when talking to the boys, and this was now forbidden. To many, if not most, it seemed as if the new man was making a mountain out of a molehill, but the more perceptive and sensitive may have been able to see that to conform to the boys' own evaluation of themselves as members of a different order was to maintain the hitherto unbridgeable gap between 'we' and 'they'; the moral superior 'we', and the outcast criminal 'they'.

Balbernie tried to explain what lay behind this approach and the reasons for it. The need for a good model of masculinity with which to identify and to show what manliness really is I have referred to. He now reminded them that these boys were not merely rejected by society as delinquents and misfits; many of them had at an earlier age been woefully rejected by those who in happier circumstances would have loved them most, and deep down they felt themselves to be unwanted, worthless, useless failures. Their building of a delinquent society of their own in which they might find acceptance (by enduring manfully the pains of the initiation rites) and the sense of achievement (by fighting for a higher place in the pecking order) was a pathetic attempt – vicious though it might be – to compensate for earlier rejection and its accompanying sense of failure. In the subculture, acceptance could be sought and indeed found by nothing more difficult than enduring pain, but acceptance by rejecting parents or by society had proved more difficult to achieve. What they must have now was real acceptance instead of rejection, instead of the sham acceptance of the subculture, instead of finding security by striving to become what they most feared. Total acceptance of themselves as they were, with their perverted sense of values, with their hatred, their nasty habits and their foul temper. Acceptance (and this was difficult to understand) of the person who expressed himself in these horrible and revolting ways, but not of the way in which he expressed himself. The deeds must be condemned but not the doer. We learn best from people who accept and like us, but rejection evokes reciprocal rejection, rejection of all the teacher has to teach as well as of the teacher. In the old system of two sides, we and they, staff and boys, goodies and baddies, moral precepts were largely wasted because they were uttered by people associated in the boys' minds with the rejectors, and were therefore in their turn rejected. But when a child feels in his bones that a person has accepted him, that person can condemn his behaviour with the greatest sternness; only now, as the moral precepts come from an accepting person, there is at least some chance that those precepts will be accepted. Not perhaps immediately, and not perhaps acted on forthwith, but when in time the boy begins to acquire a real identity (as a result of his experiences at the Community) – real 'ego strength' – then perhaps he will act on those precepts. Not only on those precepts, but on all that he has seen, admired and identified himself with in the way in which the adults around him look at life. That is why those people have to be real men of integrity and personal concern.

All this was not only difficult to understand, it was fatally easy to misunderstand, and it was especially easy to misunderstand by any who did not particularly want to understand it. Very easy to misunderstand too by people living in the vicinity, who had been neighbours to Cotswold School for more than a quarter of a century, and who now heard accounts (some of them embroidered) of how under the new management the boys did just as they pleased – 'There's no control any more – they're simply taking the place apart' – and so on. All this had to be, and, indeed, has been weathered. Time and again Balbernie had to assert that there was no room for woolly permissiveness. The fact that we accept and approve of a boy as a person and that we do not punish him for his misdeeds does most emphatically not mean that we give him a licence to do just as he pleases. These unstable, damaged, delinquent boys need – especially when they first arrive – firm control for their own protection and the protection of others. But control (and how incredibly difficult it is to get this point home) need not, and at Cotswold certainly would not, mean a system of rules, prohibitions and punishments. It means making the boundaries perfectly clear – boundaries in space, in time, in behaviour – intervening when there is an illicit attempt to cross those boundaries, or better when such an attempt is contemplated, and within those boundaries creating an atmosphere of concern and safety. A child who knows for sure what the boundaries are, who feels that his environing adults are concerned about him and respect him, who is rebuked when need arises without equivocation but without animosity – such a child feels secure, and the impulse to misbehaviour is by so much the less. The boundaries will be tested, and the adults will be tested. That is to be expected and suffered and dealt with in a mature realistic way, and not by resorting to panic or to temper or to any other childish reaction. No one suggested that any of this was easy, and of course it is immeasurably more difficult and demanding than the old routine of punishments and grades and 'discipline'. But it was the way the Cotswold Community was going to be run, and anyone who found it too difficult had better find himself a job where things were easier.

This is the kind of thing Balbernie was saying in those early staff meetings, supplementing it with cyclostyled memoranda and with teaching films.* He was saying it to a staff which seemed at first largely uncomprehending, some of whom were hurt and perplexed, some resentful and some contemptuously hostile. Some however – perhaps not more than four or five but certainly *some* – understood from the start what he was after, welcomed it and even, with great courage, came out into the open in support of the new approach. And it did require courage, because it was much easier for the hostile group to vent their animosity directly on them than on the principal, and some did not hesitate to do so.

At the same time it was necessary to demonstrate the change to the boys, and he instituted Community meetings, once or sometimes twice a week, which everyone – staff and boys – was required to attend. There was to be no more 'we' and 'they'. They were a community of people living together, and all that happened in that community was everybody's concern. They would meet together and anyone was at liberty to say anything about anything. 'A mad thing to do,' he said to me somewhat ruefully two years later, responding perhaps to my look of incredulity rather than to anything I said. But it was the only thing to do at the time. It was imperative that he should go at

---

*The films used included the Robertsons' *John* and *Jane*, each graphically illustrating the effect on young children of separation from parents. *A Two Year Old Goes to Hospital* deals with the same theme. A Canadian film called *The Feeling of Hostility* shows the effect upon current behaviour of earlier emotional experiences. An American film *Angry Boy* deals with cooperation between residential and field workers involved with the same family. Balbernie thinks the two most useful were the UNESCO film *The Quiet One*, which shows how a withdrawn boy drifts into delinquency and how he is helped by good residential treatment; and the Lippitt Whyte film *Record*, which compares and contrasts various modes of conducting groups in a youth-club setting.

it like a bull at a gate. If he had attempted to go gently and slowly, introducing changes gradually, here and there, the great probability is that the long continued tensions and resentments would have overwhelmed him. It was essential that he should make the break total and drastic at the very beginning, though the community he hoped to see would be a matter for slow building.

The Community meetings went on for eight or nine weeks until he had made his main point and everyone had got the measure of the new man. They were – for him at any rate – periods of acute tension and distress. Not for one moment must it be assumed that the boys saw in this new man with his crazy ideas a saviour. They saw in him, as I have said, someone who was upsetting the familiar applecart. Many of the adults were in a state of fury about a situation in which mere delinquent kids were encouraged to say what they liked about their elders and betters without even being told not to be impertinent. The only consolation was that they too were free to say what they liked, but they found this as difficult as the boys did. The boys at first were naturally sceptical about the new man's intentions and motives but they had plenty to say during the first two meetings. What they said had little direct connection with the proposed changes, but was largely in the nature of grouses about the regime as they had experienced it hitherto – grouses about food, about pocket money, about smoking. Most of this was 'surface stuff' but to the knowledgeable much of it was tied up with the power and influence of the tobacco trade among the boys. Smoking had been allowed only at certain very limited times (though of course as always in such circumstances it was commonly recognized that it was going on in secret all the time) and the boys in the punishment grades, having very little money and no exeats, would become desperate for tobacco – tobacco not always and necessarily for themselves, but partly at least for the purpose of placating those who terrorized them. To get it they would sell anything, including themselves. This was the basis of the power of the tobacco barons, and simply liberalizing the regulations concerning pocket money and smoking did much to break their pernicious rule.

Staff and boys were invited to form committees to work out

what was needed in the way of altering internal regulations and arrangements, and one or two adults did join with small groups of boys for this purpose. They eventually produced some very good, well-worked-out schemes. They made, for example, more effective and rational regulations about the use of tobacco, thus attacking one of the evils that had been at the heart of the subculture; they reorganized the serving of food in the dining-room so that bullies could not impose 'food taxes'; and they made constructive suggestions about work payments.

It was at the third meeting that the first crisis came. For some reason that has never come clearly to light word had come from the centres of power – presumably from the leaders of the underground tyranny – that boys were not to speak at Community meetings; and no boys spoke. This was clearly a trial of strength between the new principal and the old subculture. The meeting endured for nearly an hour in perfect silence, then almost at the end a brave boy spoke. He spoke clearly and lucidly, and the main part of what he had to say concerned the danger to any boys who ventured to speak. Balbernie in turn spoke with the utmost vehemence of the dangers – emanating from him – to anyone who presumed so much as to lay a hand on or faintly victimize anyone who spoke at a meeting, and he does not think this boy was touched.

The staff were reluctant to say much for a reason which was basically the same. After all Balbernie was the boss, in close touch with the managers who had hiring and firing powers, and who was to know what his reactions might be to someone who was openly critical? However, in spite of this general reluctance to speak, personal animosity against the principal found biting expression from time to time.

'Is it right,' said a boy, 'for staff children to shoot the Community's birds?'

'Well,' said Balbernie. 'Is it? What do you – any of you – think?'

'Mr Priestman says . . . ,' began the boy.

'Never mind what Mr Priestman says. He's here and quite capable of speaking for himself. You speak for *yourself*. Tell us what it's all about and then we can hear what people think about it.'

The sad and shabby story soon came out. Balbernie's twelve-year-old son had an old handed-down airgun, of very limited power and range. With this he would amuse himself in the garden of the principal's house, potting at tin lids suspended from the branches of trees, perhaps even at the odd bird. If by some fluke the pellet or dart had actually reached a bird it would have been so spent that it would have done no damage anyway. Balbernie did not say all this. He did not suppose that the boy or the man was really concerned about the Community's birds; he suspected that their purpose was simply to be awkward to himself, Balbernie and his family. He knew too that they were all victims of the pernicious, unrealistic split between 'goodies' and 'baddies'. The Community boys were of course the baddies – they must be, or they wouldn't be there – and all others were goodies. There was no in-between state in this iron division; all who were not baddies must be goodies, and the principal's son was not 'allowed' to have any normal boyish faults. He *must* be a goodie, and, seeing whose son he was, a super-goodie, as beyond reproach as Caesar's wife. This totally unreal black-and-white classification was one of the things Balbernie was out to destroy, but that would take time. What he did say was that he could hardly answer for his son in this matter, but that there was no reason why he should not answer for himself. He would, if they wished, send for the boy, and he could come to the meeting and answer their charges. A vote was taken on the question, 'Who thinks we should send for him?' but not a single boy or man raised his hand. He then told them that much against his parents' wishes the boy was shortly going away to a boarding school because life at home had been made intolerable for him by boys of the Community. A gang of them had persistently hounded him, pursuing him about the property and threatening him with violence. He once escaped actual bodily harm only because by a happy chance his father came upon him surrounded by a taunting threatening mob and was able to rescue him. That very morning this same gang had assaulted another boy, beating him up and knocking out several of his front teeth.

There was little constructive discussion at these meetings. Balbernie had not really expected there would be. They were far too large for the kind of therapeutic group that was later to become a feature of the Community, but they did serve the purpose of making clear to everyone what manner of man he was, and of giving some inkling at least of the way he intended the Community to develop.

I have had a great deal of experience of community meetings and I would not have had the courage to do as Balbernie did. He told me they were pure hell. When each meeting finished he felt so utterly destroyed that it would take all the intervening days to summon up the strength and courage enough to face another. He kept them up for a couple of months, and my admiration for this achievement is boundless.

# 3 Beginning the New

So far then the new principal had done two things, which amounted together to little more than a declaration of intent. He had kicked away the bases of the old system and said what he would not have in the future; and had given some kind of general indication of the kind of philosophy which was to be the foundation on which he hoped to build. It was now necessary to create the conditions in which that building could begin, and a more daunting task it would be difficult to conceive. He saw two immediate major problems.

The first, and less difficult, was the problem of management structure. This involved changes in staff roles and attitudes that were so drastic and seemed so novel to those long accustomed to different ways that they needed a great deal of explanation to the staff, who accepted them no more easily than the other changes with which they were integrally linked; and they call for comment here.

Perhaps the change that was most difficult to understand and to accept was in the role and function of the head. The structure he had inherited was perhaps well suited to achieve maximum efficiency in the system he was engaged in replacing. It was a pyramidal structure with the headmaster at the top, the ultimate source of all power, responsibility, knowledge, information. He alone knew everything, initiated everything, controlled everything in detail. Nothing was done without his permission, his signature, his initials in the appropriate column. He was the god of this little world, and that was indeed the name by which in my borstal days we used to refer to the governor. It happens that while I was writing these lines a speaker in a television feature about borstal earned for himself a rebuke from borstal officials by saying that the authoritarian, regimented power structure of borstal attracted to its staff men who were like sheep. It was perhaps an unfortunate simile and I think was misunderstood. He meant, presumably, that such a system

attracts good, loyal, orthodox, obedient carriers-out of instructions who will thus tend to rely on those instructions, following directions rather than being self-reliant and finding their
own way. If the aim is to encourage self-reliance, initiative,
independence and the exercise of a personal, inward authority
in all ranks – and this was now the aim at the Cotswold – then
the borstal kind of structure would not do. The god-like image
of the head was further enhanced by the presence of a deputy
and a 'third in charge'. The deputy's function (he said) was to
oil the wheels and see that everything ran smoothly; so that it
was possible to get the impression that the primary task of
everybody concerned was at all costs to *keep* this machinery
running smoothly, irrespective of whether it actually produced
the almost forgotten end for which it had been created; the
means seemed to have become the end. One is reminded of a
remark made many years ago by Barnett of Toynbee Hall, and
recorded by Stephen Hobhouse, to whom he made it. He said:
'The idea creates the organization, but we must beware that the
organization does not destroy the idea.' This ever-present danger
is one of which the present leadership of the Community is
acutely aware.

Apart from his monopoly of authority in the sense of control,
the head also enjoyed (if that is the right word) a monopoly of
authority in the academic sense of being the person who knows
everything. But whereas such a person is usually an authority
in one field only, his was the last word in matters of education,
of crafts and skills, of child care and social work, of therapy –
even of farming, horticulture and estate management. This
implies a mastery of diverse skills which no man possesses, and
which the new principal would have been the last to claim.

It is much to Balbernie's credit that he never hesitated to seek
advice, and he had sought advice on the complex and perplexing
problem of what organizational arrangements were best suited
to the carrying out of the Community's new task. This problem
was clearly one for the Tavistock Institute of Human Relations,
and to them, with the help and approval of the Rainer Foundation, he had gone. Theirs was to be a continuing assessment of
the exact task of the Community, beginning with a preliminary
appraisal of needs, and a design for the best way of meeting

those needs. The Institute appointed to this project Mr Kenneth Rice. His first report, *Working Note No. 1*, ran into something like fifty typewritten pages, and was followed three months later (in May 1968) by a much shorter *Working Note No. 2*. Dr Eric Miller was also closely involved for a time, and gave much valuable help. One of the many calamities that the Community had to suffer was that Kenneth Rice, who had a profound understanding of, and sympathy with, the aims and ideals of the Community, died while still in his middle years. However the Institute was able eventually to make other arrangements, and appointed Miss Isabel Menzies to continue the work. Her *Working Note No. 3* was produced in June 1970. It is not my purpose to summarize these reports; their findings, in so far as they have been implemented, will find their appropriate place in my narrative.

In the Community, as elsewhere, there are two main and quite separate aspects of a person's life – his home and his work. In ordinary life these are quite separate from each other with clearly defined boundaries which everyone consciously crosses every day. These boundaries, if his Community experience was to help to prepare a boy for life, should be equally well drawn there. *Working Note No. 1* distinguished clearly between them, calling the home-life aspect of the Community 'group living', and dividing the work aspect again into two – school and employment. In the latter aspect it insisted that boundaries should be equally clear, that school should be school and work should be proper, realistic, economics-based employment. In the event, the number of boys for whom employment in that sense seemed a proper and fruitful arrangement turned out to be very few indeed.

The first change in the staff structure was to 'chop off' the top of the power pyramid by abolishing the posts of deputy and third in charge altogether, and totally changing the role of the head, making him an enabler and facilitator rather than a director. Authority and responsibility was then distributed among four people with entirely different and separate areas of interest and skill, each of whom was responsible for his own sphere, with no crossing of boundaries. One man was to be in charge of the home life of the Community – head of group living; one was in charge of the school and the trade-training departments – head of education; a third was in charge of financial affairs, of estate management and the maintenance of the fabric – the bursar; and the fourth, a woman, was to be in charge of all domestic arrangements (operating in this sphere through a domestic bursar) and the specific therapeutic duties of the housemothers. These four came to be known as 'first-line management'. Their spheres, their boundaries, were clear and well defined, and their authority within those boundaries absolute. They met together every morning at 8.30 a.m. with the principal to exchange information, and to coordinate activities. (I attended one of these meetings during one of my earlier visits, and found them discussing the sordid subject of refuse, rubble, debris, garbage. The debris and rubbish about the place were due partly to the physical process of change during which buildings were being quickly adapted to different uses, and partly to the vandalism of the boys during the initial period of disorder. It was thought that the time had now been reached when it might be possible to get on top of this problem, and I listened to the discussion wondering whether the plans then being made would actually and effectively be put into operation. By my next visit, a month later, the place had been transformed, and has remained so. These people were not woolly idealists: they were competent, efficient, practical professionals.)

It was assumed that each of these four would cultivate with his own colleagues the kind of relationship which the principal now had with *them*, namely that so far as possible each man's job would have its own clear boundaries within which he is master, free to use his own particular skills and gifts in his own way – always assuming that he understands and accepts the essential spirit and purpose which was now to animate the Community. By this means the task of the Community became the individual personal task of every man and woman, whereas hitherto it had been in effect the task only of the head, on whose behalf all these others had been working.

It will readily be seen that the discontented and subversive would immediately accuse the new principal of shirking his responsibilities and leaving himself with a sinecure. *That* he had to suffer in addition to the mortification and extreme self-discipline of standing back while others plunged into work, which in some cases it would have been foolish to pretend he could not have done better. Leadership in this sense, as developing the gifts, capacities, understanding and authority of others, rather than directing and controlling their efforts, he saw as his specific task. This aspect of it – the standing back and holding himself in – was probably the most wearisome, distressing and frustrating of all the burdens he had to bear during these early days. The only means by which most of the staff could get a grasp of the head's new place in the scheme of things was in a practical way, by probing and pushing and 'trying it on' and in general testing him in every way possible. It was indeed necessary, before things could be stabilized (necessary perhaps even in helping *him* to get into his role), that he should be tested in this way, as the jargon saying is, 'to destruction' – and that testing certainly took place. To those who stupidly or maliciously assumed that all this left the principal with a cushy job, there was nothing that could effectively be said. This for the time being simply had to be borne. The source of Balbernie's real anxiety, amounting at times almost to anguish, was those good, able, loyal men who began to see the virtues of the new way and who, while not yet understanding it, were anxious – being the kind of men they were – to do their best to cooperate. These men constantly sought to be directed in the old sense, and it was the principal's duty constantly to 'fail' them as director and controller. If I may repeat the image of the television speaker as Milton used it, the hungry sheep looked up and were not fed. Their reproaches were immeasurably harder to bear than the jibes of the mischief makers, but they too had to be borne. It would have been simple, as it would have been extremely satisfying, for Balbernie to rush in everywhere, directing, changing, controlling, adjusting, showing how it should be done – and creating another omnipotent figure of a different kind, to the ultimate miscarriage of all he was working towards. We have all seen parents watching their infants at some childish ploy – building something with bricks, clambering over an obstacle or something of that kind. The instinctive impulse of the parent is to help, to do the construction, to lift the child over the obstacle. But the wise parent waits, because she knows that the child learns more, acquires greater self-confidence, becomes more of a person, if he is left to solve his own problems. It is no disparagement of Balbernie's colleagues to suggest that his relationship with them at this time was very much the same, and he had to exercise the patience and self-restraint of the wise parent. This does not mean total withdrawal or lack of concern; the mother's continued presence and occasional word of encouragement enables the child to succeed; the wise parent will intervene to prevent disaster or unbearable frustration. It was an immensely difficult and subtle role in which the principal was cast, between an inhibiting oversight on the one hand and a frightening withdrawal on the other. Inasmuch as it was essential to eliminate the dependence that had hitherto characterized the staff in general, any error, any leaning too far one way or the other, had to be rather on the side of withdrawal than its opposite, or a new kind of dependency might be created. In his own words, he saw his job as 'moving consciously and carefully in response to the music behind the scenes', and I can describe it no better.

We come now to the second of the two main problems to which I referred. It was one thing to tell the staff in broad terms what the new approach was to be, but another thing altogether to get them to understand and accept it. Even if that were achieved, it was still another thing to convey to them how in practical detail it affected their day-to-day intimate contacts with the boys. Such of them as were teachers had been trained as teachers; the trade instructors were fully qualified to practise their crafts, but had little training in teaching them; some, but not all, of the housemasters had at some time taken the Home Office certificate in residential child care. But none of them – teachers, instructors, house-staff – had been given any real and thorough training in the specific task of applying environmental therapy to disturbed, unstable, deprived and delinquent boys. Few, if any, had had any teaching about the dynamics of human behaviour and the development of the personality. Few, if any, had any knowledge or understanding of the tensions and emotionally charged interactions that can animate a group of people. On the contrary they had worked, some of them for the best part of a lifetime, in a system and an atmosphere that was quite inimical to the new approach, and they had a perfectly proper and understandable loyalty to the old ways. Their own needs compelled these men to attach moral worth to the old way, and generated in some a blind unreasoning and fierce hostility to the new. Perhaps some might be given a little understanding of their own unconscious motives and helped to learn how to seek different satisfactions, but the number was not likely to be great.

These two groups, the hostile and the bewildered, constituted the large majority of the staff. How could they possibly be brought to the point where they could be of any use in the new regime? The only hope was that the remainder might be educable. But education, re-education, training, advice must be made available for all, and this Balbernie now set out to provide. Apart from the chaplain, a staunch supporter from the beginning, who now took over the function of bursar in addition to his spiritual duties, one man alone was definitely known at the beginning to be wholly committed to the new approach. This was Trevor Blewett, a young (thirty-ish) teacher who had worked in the old regime for a couple of years, found it wanting, and had gone off to get further training at an advanced course for residential workers. Appraised of the impending changes, Blewett returned eagerly to the Community when his course finished, just about the time that Balbernie arrived there. To him, when Rice had submitted his report and the new staff structure began to be effected, was given the job of head of group living.

It was fortunate that Balbernie had been for some years engaged in the academic and research aspects of child care and therapy, in addition to his experience as teacher, psychologist, psychotherapist and head of a school for maladjusted children. He had a wide circle of acquaintance in the field, and knew where to look for help. The people he called upon were for the most part colleagues and personal friends, and it was at first on a personal, rather than a professional, basis that they willingly came to his aid. It was important to get them in quickly; he got them in, and made formal arrangements with his employers and the Home Office in the fullness of time. They were all people who were not only highly skilled and experienced, they were all deeply concerned for the work that was now being done at the Cotswold Community.

The help they gave was in two particular areas, though they

are areas with a large overlap. There was the area of personal relationships between adults and children, which involves not only an understanding of child development (and maldevelopment) but also the effect on the feelings – and hence the behaviour – of each, brought about by the interactions between child and adult. The other area in which learning was essential was the whole field of group dynamics. The Community was to be split up into small self-contained groups. It was important that the adults living in them should know something about personal interactions within a group, what personal and communal feelings are likely to be aroused, and how they can be exploited to therapeutic ends.

To help in the first area (though the extent of the overlap must never be forgotten) he was able to call on his friends of many years, Mrs Barbara Dockar-Drysdale and Mr Michael Fitzgerald. Mrs Dockar-Drysdale is a psychotherapist who is widely known in this country and abroad for her exciting work at the Mulberry Bush School, a well-known and highly esteemed school for maladjusted children, which she and her husband founded and ran for twenty years or more. Fitzgerald, after working for some years with George Lyward and later as inspector in the LCC Children's Department, is now consultant in residential child care to several London boroughs. The enormous virtue of these distingushed consultants, in this particular context, was that they could not be accused of being vague, impractical theorists. They had 'done their stuff' over many years right down at the grass roots in difficult residential situations, and could relate academic theory to the practical problems of the man on the job as well as translating academic and psychiatric jargon into everyday speech.

Fitzgerald came to the Community once a fortnight and conducted what we may think of as a seminar with the staff of one of the houses. He did valuable work for a time but was unable to continue indefinitely. Mrs Dockar-Drysdale however has a permanent appointment as therapeutic consultant, and her contribution has been and is invaluable. She spends one whole very busy and (I should imagine) exhausting day at the Community each week, and on my visits I heard constant references by all manner of people to the value to them of her work. My visits were of course made later than the period of which I am now writing, when Mrs Dockar-Drysdale's first task was to get herself accepted by a staff many of whom were, to say the least, sceptical. That she was successful in this – and so quickly successful – is perhaps the best tribute that can be paid.

To the staff of each living unit in turn she gives a very crowded hour, in which they bring forward for discussion anything whatever about which they are perplexed. And when I say 'bring forward for discussion' I mean just that, for the consultant sees her role not as giving answers to questions, but as helping people to find their own answers if answers are to be found. The questions raised may call for an examination and interpretation of a child's behaviour, and they may equally call for examination and interpretation of the behaviour of an adult. Sometimes the meeting will take the form of a case conference about a particular boy, and sometimes it may take the form of a 'context profile'. This fascinating and enlightening process is one which Mrs Dockar-Drysdale has evolved, and I was allowed to sit in on one. It provides a more accurate picture of the state of a child's feelings and relationships at a given moment in time than any other method known to me, and consists of the reporting not of impressions and opinions, but experiences. On this particular occasion every adult who had had active contact with the child under discussion during a given twenty-four hours reported in full on the actual experience of that contact, beginning with the person who awakened him in the morning and going right through to the person who tucked him up at night – and later if there was any subsequent contact. When these experiences of contact with the boy were discussed, and so far as possible interpreted and related to each other, each adult gained an overall picture of the child; a picture much freer than usual of prejudice, bias or false impressions. The child is seen in the round, and in his relations to everyone. What is more, the percipient adult learns something not only about the child but also about himself, and self-knowledge is essential to any who attempt to do therapeutic work with disturbed children.*

* Mrs Dockar-Drysdale has written about context profiles (among other things) in her book *Therapy in Child Care*, Longman, 1969.

In addition to her sessions with the four staff groups, the therapeutic consultant also makes herself available to any staff-member who wants to see her privately, and even finds time occasionally to interview a child.

Mrs Dockar-Drysdale, then, is the permanent therapeutic consultant, but other consultants and advisers have been made available from time to time on a temporary or occasional basis – Dr Marcus Lipton and Dr Marquette, for example, of the Tavistock Clinic, and Mr Arthur Barron, a psychotherapist, who also has had many years of residential experience, and is a trustee of the Planned Environment Therapy Trust.

In the area of group dynamics the Tavistock Institute seemed the obvious resource, but it was more practical to make use of facilities of a similar kind closer at hand, at Bristol University, where Balbernie had himself worked. Those who teach group dynamics claim that the only way to undersand them is to experience them, and they are 'taught' therefore through the medium of what is called a study group. Here the students meet with a consultant or adviser to examine what is happening in the sphere of feelings and interactions in the group which they now constitute, and particularly the interactions between group and leader. After several meetings as a study group they may then meet as an application group which, as its name implies, looks at the application of what has been and is being learned to the day-to-day work of the students. Several senior staff members were therefore attached to a study group meeting weekly in Bristol, and before very long Mr Philip Kingston came weekly from Bristol to conduct a study group with other staff members at the Community. Mr Christopher Holtom also came in a consultant capacity to advise the head of group living, and to conduct a seminar with the staff of one of the houses, discussing staff roles and leadership in the context of group living, as well as sometimes conducting study groups. Mr Holtom, again, has had years of experience with delinquents in a residential setting, and was at that time engaged in the training of probation officers.

The principal was not without personal consultant help. He was in a very lonely, exposed and vulnerable position and it was essential both that he should be able to get objective comments on the work in general and that he should be able, so far as possible, to keep his mind perfectly clear about what he was doing – and perhaps also about what it was doing to him! To these ends he received much help from Kenneth Rice, and from Mrs A. I. Allenby, an analytical psychologist with many years of residential experience. But this was, so to speak, behind the scenes; what we are really concerned about at the moment is the arrangements for trying to give the staff in general a clearer idea of all that lay behind the new approach.

These arrangements received, as can be imagined, a mixed reception from those for whose benefit they were made. Some, impervious to any kind of approach that was made to them, persisted in regarding it all as unadulterated nonsense; some looked at these new ideas with minds as open as they could make them, and with every intention of examining them without prejudice, but sadly shook their heads in lack of comprehension. From a few, however – and these not necessarily the younger men – the ideas that now began to circulate evoked a positive response. The fact emerged, after a few months, that there *were* men who although they had cooperated loyally in the old regime, had done so not because they thought it ideal, or because it was the kind of thing they had expected when they joined the service, but just because they were conscientious and loyal, and had never been shown any other way. The old way was, so far as their experience had gone, the only way, and they were now delighted to find that the real concern they felt for the boys was after all not something to be inhibited and even perhaps despised, but something which should be expressed and communicated, and without which indeed no therapy was possible.

One such man, Mr Glyn Jones, said to me some thirty months after the changeover, 'In the old days you were given your job and left to get on with it. If you made a mistake you were told off. But now, you have your job, but you're given some idea how to go about it. You have a chance to learn, and to talk about it with people who understand. In the old days, I wasn't what you could really call unhappy. It was a job, you did your stint of duty hours each day, then you went home and tried to forget about it. But now I am really happy. I get real satisfaction out of my job, which was a thing I never got before.' He told me

how effects of the new regime first began to be seen in the boys'
deportment. He said they seemed to be happier – genuinely
happy, and not superficially happy. It is difficult to convey in
print what he conveyed to me – with real feeling – in words.
'In the old days you'd arrive at work in the morning and any
boys you happened to pass would say, "Morning, Mr Jones."
After Richard Balbernie had been here a little while you'd have
them saying, "Good morning." ' The first 'Morning, Mr Jones' had
been a stiff and formal, if not sullen utterance of something that
discipline and good order required of them. The other 'Good
morning', had been a spontaneous and cheerful expression of
good will. Mr Jones did not say all that, but conveyed it most
vividly in his mimicry of the two different greetings. 'Then,' he
said, 'they started doing something that would have been absolutely unthinkable before – they started behaving like boys. I'd
be walking down the drive on my way to work and two or
three of them would be waiting to waylay me. They'd spring
out of hiding with a shout to startle me, then drop alongside
and walk on with me.' Such a little thing but, as this sensitive
man who had worked for years under the old regime was able
to see, what a world of meaning it contained; how horrifying
to think that for years such natural, spontaneous behaviour had
been 'unthinkable'. And when I speak of him as a sensitive man,
I do not wish to conjure up a picture of a 'sensitive', willowy
aesthete out of touch with the facts of life. This was a burly,
manly man, a builder by trade, who was able to present to the
boys the image and model of strong masculine concern for
others which was so necessary to counteract the immature,
childish image of masculinity which had so far been the dreadful
model of most of them.

Mr Glyn Jones's recollections remind us that while Rice was
making his study, while Balbernie was seeking and bringing in
advisers and consultants, the ordinary life of the Community had
still to be carried on. We have seen how those staff members
who were frankly hostile to the change were prevented from
open collusion with disorder by fear of losing their jobs; they
might have been able to drive Balbernie away, but if they had
done so they would have had to go with him. Nevertheless disorder there was, and was bound to be when the old kind of

authority had had its main supports removed, and the staff –
however willing – had not yet learned how to wield the new
one. There was disorder, there was aggression, there was damage
to property. The old authority had kept the boy's primitive
aggression sufficiently under control to keep property intact,
but now it began to erupt in senseless, anonymous vandalism.
Paint was splashed about, stones would come hurtling from
nowhere, windows would be broken, all confirming the fears of
those staff members who had not only predicted it and perhaps
welcomed it, but who assumed that under the new regime this
kind of thing must inevitably go on indefinitely. But of course
it did not. Balbernie felt it to be inevitable and indeed necessary
that the boys should test the new regime 'to destruction' in
order to prove what it was really made of. When the unfailing
care and concern that were replacing discipline and punishment
began to be felt, and were clearly seen to be surviving this
terrible testing, then the destructive acting out came to an end.

It would have come to an end sooner if all the staff, from the
very beginning, had fully understood and sympathized with the
new approach. In the meantime the subculture continued to
flourish, but was at fewer pains to keep itself out of sight.
Balbernie, hearing of trouble one evening in one of the houses,
went over there to find a scene of gross disorder. Everything
was saturated with water, and on one of the beds was a vest that
was saturated with blood. At the centre of the maelstrom of
yelling boys was a whimpering child whose face had been 'bat-
tered to a pulp'. This small boy was so consumed by terror that
he was totally unable to speak. Balbernie confesses that he was
frightened himself – as who would not have been? – especially
when it seemed that some of the bigger boys intended violence
to him. But he put on a bold front and some kind of order was
restored. He then expressed himself very forcibly to the housemaster, giving his opinion of people who allowed disorder and
violence to develop to the point where suffering of that kind
could be inflicted on a boy. The bully who had been the leader
of this sadistic attack was transferred almost overnight to
another institution, but that in itself was no solution to the
problem of violence and the passing on to each new boy who
came the infection of the subculture. The older boys who were

doing the bullying had once themselves been new boys who were bullied, and it was essential that some effort be made to check this infection, quite apart from the cognate question of establishing the physical safety of the smaller and newer boys.

To begin with, the 'irrecoverable' boys were got rid of. These were boys who had already been at the school a year or so, and had become so deeply infected – in addition to whatever had been their problems when they had first arrived – that there was simply no hope of doing anything with them in the short remaining time that it was feasible to keep them. Not only that, but these were the boys who 'ran' the subculture, the protection rackets, the initiation ceremonies, the sexual horrors. It was recognized that as soon as those boys left others would aspire to their privileges, but it was thought that perhaps that could be dealt with. One of the astonishing and tragic things that emerged at this time was that in some strange way the boys seemed to *need* the institutional culture with its rituals and rankings, its brutish sexual customs, its ruthless economic empires. They clung to it, in Balbernie's words, like a small boy clings to his teddy bear. This was the reality they knew, horrible though it may have been, and it had tangible rewards for those who could 'make the grade'. But even for those who could not hope to reach the top, it was *there*, it was the actual life they had to live, and one had to accommodate to it and get the most one could out of it. It provided, for all its enormities, a kind of order, a kind of security, and even the mildest and most ordinary boys got caught up in it and identified with it in much the same way as the boys in *The Lord of the Flies*. In so far as the boys were being influenced by their environment – and it was for this purpose they had come there – *this* was the environment that was influencing them. Its dominion was so complete that no other influences could effectually reach them, and that dominion had to be broken if they were to be made accessible to the influences it was hoped might now be brought to bear. So the irrecoverables had to go, and within six months of the takeover some fifty boys had been discharged; by May 1968 the nominal roll was down to fifty-three.

These reduced numbers facilitated the drastic rearrangements that were now planned. The whole of the hundred or so boys had lived, as we have seen, closely packed together round the 'back square'. True, they were in separate houses, but nevertheless the Community was in effect one dense unit – even though a few boys were in a new building outside the square which had been built as a 'pre-release' house. It was essential that the boys should be split up into small separate living groups, at a distance from each other, each with its own adults and its own clearly defined spatial boundaries, with a good deal of autonomy under the guiding influence of the head of group living. Balbernie had been much interested in the work of Konrad Lorenz, and in this context his book *Aggression* is of particular relevance. No one can have read this fascinating book without coming to question the common assumption that aggressiveness is something of which everyone has a reservoir which must from time to time be discharged. To the creatures Lorenz studied it was something closely connected with territory. It was for the most part in defence of territory that they became aggressive (though surprisingly often in only a token way) and it seemed to be the possession of territory that gave them identity and made them real 'persons'. At the Cotswold now each group of boys was to have its own territory, and each child could then begin to feel the safety and security that boundaries provide. Not walls or fences, but boundaries. Not, 'You are forbidden to go beyond there', but 'This area is our own. Here we are at home'; boundaries that would have to be crossed, and consciously crossed, to go to school, to go to work, to go anywhere. Every staff member, whatever his primary function, would be allocated to one of these groups, as a main resource or as a part-time resource.

I find I am falling into the jargon. It is difficult to avoid after a few days spent at the Community, and although it infuriates me, and for at least forty-eight hours one is often uncertain what people are talking about, I also find it rather appealing. It is a mixture derived from several sources – the group-dynamics people at the Tavistock Centre, the management experts at the same place, psychopathology and psychiatry (two parts of Jung to three of Freud), academic psychology, the growing field of child-care training, and probably others that I have not yet identified. I tried to tease them about it when I first went there but found they did not take kindly to my teasing, so I dropped it. But whatever else it may mean, this extensively used Cotswold jargon does mean that there is a vitality and a life and a culture that have infected everyone who lives there. However, that stage had not been reached.

Within these boundaries it would be possible for genuine adult–child relationships to develop, based on concern rather than 'control'; and the kind of regimentation essential when you are dealing with masses would no longer be needed. A survey was therefore begun of available buildings on the estate, buildings which could be adapted, or whose use could be changed. Plans began to emerge for the dispersal of living groups around the place, but so far as there was a plan it was purely tentative, to be put into operation as soon as possible but necessarily in stages. Money had to be found for adaptations, other accommodation had to be found for present occupants, alterations had to be made and decoration done; for the new group homes were to *be* homes, and not the bare ruined barracks of the past.

Rice's *Working Note No. 1* envisaged the continuance of the present houses in the sense that each group would be attached to a notional 'house' under a house warden to whom the group leaders would be responsible. I must say that this never struck me as being a very realistic kind of design, and in fact it has never materialized, though Balbernie thinks there may be a place for it with a certain kind of boy. The people at the Cotswold are always ready to recognize their errors, and as they have kept a running record of plans, thoughts, impressions and proposals from the very beginning, they have all their false judgements and erroneous impressions constantly before them – a very salutary exercise! One of their earlier assumptions was that if only they could free the boys of the overlay of institutional culture – both formal and illicit – they would find beneath that overlay some fairly normal people. This assumption rather surprises me, but it does show how willing they were to listen to what the old approved-school hands had to say. Among them there is an appreciable number who incline to the view that many if not most delinquent boys are simply boys who have been allowed to run wild, have not been properly trained and

controlled by their parents, and just need a little good whole-
some discipline and training in good habits to set them on the
right road again. There may be such boys, and if so they may
well be basically 'normal'; but I doubt whether very many of
them get into approved schools. In the scheme envisaged on
this assumption, the younger men would have something like
a peer relationship (one might almost say a big-brother relationship if that phrase had not accumulated so many unhappy
associations), and the older man, chosen from among those who
already had considerable status in the old hierarchy, would
provide the adult examplar so much needed by adolescent boys.

Unhappily they found beneath that overlay not fairly normal
boys whose relatively simple needs could be met by such an
arrangement, but a collection of boys most of whom were to a
greater or lesser degree maladjusted, and some of whom were
suffering from deep emotional disturbance. They were the sort of
boys Balbernie had met in his work with maladjusted children
except that they had acquired what I described earlier as a
delinquent orientation. Boys for example like Ben, the son of
an unmarried girl who had promptly had him adopted. The
adoptive mother, no longer in the first flush of youth, wanted a
baby because her doctor had told her that her asthma might
improve if she had one. He was mistaken, so the baby which
had 'promised' to cure her was a fraud and she had no further
use for him. From an early age he sought the affection she
denied him by wandering about, and frequently had to be
fetched from distant police stations. The adoptive father was
well intentioned but inadequate, and was completely tyrannized
(as Ben was) by his wife's asthma 'weapon'. He vented on Ben
the spleen he could not vent on his invalid wife. Ben was already 'hard' because he had never received affection. He now
became rebellious in reaction to his father's impotent furies,
and against all authority, frequently truanting from school and
being defiant and disorderly when he was there. It was the
combination of all these factors rather than the offence of
'breaking and entering' with other boys that was the real
reason for the approved-school order. Or like Douglas, whose
mother was not quite mad enough to be committed compulsor-

ily to a mental hospital, but so mad that her husband (who had married her to legitimize Douglas) spent all his evenings in the pub to keep out of her way; her five children were terrified by her bizarre though not necessarily unkind behaviour. She was so preoccupied with her fantasies of spectral visitations that the children were often neglected and Douglas became father and mother to the other four. Premature responsibility coupled with inadequate care made him anxious, then depressed, and he sought to escape from his depression in wild acts of daring, one of which (climbing into an empty but very tall warehouse through a roof-light) brought him to the attention of the court.

For such boys intensive work through close therapeutic relationships in a small group was essential. However that point was not yet clear and in any case the numbers of suitable staff available made the original plan more feasible than the one which ultimately emerged. Again, at this stage only one building was available outside the square, namely the one which had previously been the 'pre-release' house accommodating something like thirty boys. To this were allocated some two dozen boys with a house warden, three group leaders and a housemother. These boys were a kind of middle class – neither the very newcomers, nor the most deeply infected by the subculture – and it was hoped that Thames House, as it was now called, would be the nursery of the new approach. Here Chris Holtom came weekly to help and advise the staff, while elsewhere his colleague Philip Kingston conducted a series of study groups. In a small, tentative way, with staff finding out how to do it as they went along, the real work of the Community began to come into being, anxiously watched by those who wished and worked for its success, not less anxiously perhaps by those who longed to see it fail.

There was one serious problem, however, which was untouched by the setting up of Thames House and which needed immediate attention. It was found that some boys were more grossly disturbed and emotionally damaged than most on account of their exceptionally disrupted and deprived infancy. These were boys who from birth had never enjoyed any satisfactory relationship with a mother and who in consequence remained 'stuck' at a very primitive stage of development.

'Integrated' and 'unintegrated' were two words that had been brought to the Community by Barbara Dockar-Drysdale. As the terms are used in a more specific sense than their common use, the concept calls for a little explanation.

It arises from the belief, now pretty firmly established, that when the child is born he does not, immediately upon parturition, cease to be 'part of' the mother who bore him. They are still very much part of each other in every sense except the purely physical, and even in that sense there continues to be close and frequent contact. Certainly the child has at first no sense of 'me' and 'not me', especially in relation to his mother. Through the feeding, the loving solicitude, the tender care and attention provided by the mother, the child gradually learns to distinguish between himself and her, to establish the frail beginnings of an independent ego. The experience of these months of total reliance on the mother – called *primary* experience – enable that separation to take place, and when the independent self, the ego, is established the infant is ready and strong enough to accept all the secondary experience of growing into childhood – the little frustrations, the apprehension of what modes of conduct elicit approval, and which are frowned upon – all the things which together make for the strengthening of the ego and the growth of a real personality. The child who has been denied those early primary experiences is quite unable to accept or to make use of the secondary ones, is unable to feel anxiety or guilt, is 'frozen' (to use Mrs Dockar-Drysdale's admirably descriptive word). This is the child who is thought of as being unintegrated. He needs to experience – so far as such a thing is now possible – the primary experience he has been denied, until he is ready for the next step, is ready to learn how to accept frustration, and to develop ego strength.

Several such unintegrated boys were found to be present in the Community's population, and it was essential that they should be separated from the others into what one might think of (though never refer to!) as a kind of nursery, where they could be given as much primary experience as possible, and the kind of toleration one gives to infants. Premises were soon found that could be adapted to this use. They consisted of a long narrow concrete building which had hitherto been called the Quiet Room. In plain English it contained punishment cells,* with staff quarters used by the people who had looked after it. Here intransigent boys had been incarcerated for varying periods. It was like a small prison block, consisting of about four small rooms on each side of a narrow corridor. The windows and doors were all closely barred, the internal doors all contained judas holes so that the boys could be watched at all times. The bars were now sawn off, the judas holes papered over, comfortable furniture moved in. One room was furnished as a sitting-room, another as 'housemother's room', ostensibly for sewing and sorting out linen, but actually as a place where the 'mother' could be found employed in motherly tasks, and talked to and pestered; where above all that sense of belonging to a motherly, caring person could be generated for a time and security thereby provided. In the process of adaptation several pathetic little notes were found which had been written by boys who had been in the Quiet Room – boys perhaps who had unconsciously sought the security of being locked up just because they were the very type of uncontrolled, identity-less, unintegrated person for whom the place was now being prepared. One at least was a suicide note, though it does not appear that the would-be suicide ever found the courage – or the means? – to make his intention a reality. They were all rather suicidal and one of them reads:

I am writing this hoping that someone will find it which will be some day. LIFE IN THE SCHOOL I came here in —. My number is —. I come from London and have been there since —. I am in a quiet room which the boys call the jug. Been in number one for three weeks. [Number one was the barest and most punitive of the cells.]

* 'Separation' from other children in a 'detention room' is a recognized and permitted practice in approved schools, but is subject to careful regulation and control. It may not be used on a child under twelve, the room must be 'light and airy' and kept lighted after dark, there must be some form of occupation and a means of communication with staff. Most important, separation may not be continued for more than twenty-four hours without the written consent of a manager, in which case a written report of the circumstances must be sent immediately to the chief inspector at the Home Office.

Reason why – Mr — called me a Greek bastard so I smashed him up.*

When the Quiet Room had been converted it was renamed the Cottage, and a trained and experienced housemaster, new to Cotswold, was put in charge. With him was Pat Drew, who had recently been appointed as social-case worker and now undertook to be housemother at the Cottage until it was well established and a suitable successor could be found. Although Pat Drew is called social-case worker, her actual function at the Community is to organize the injection into this hitherto male dominion of feminine care, gentleness and intuition and all those other gifts and graces, without which life is poor and bare, and which hitherto had been lacking. In the meantime she added to her already trying task the additional one of 'mothering' the Cottage boys, both so that the Cottage could get away to a good start and also, one suspects, as some kind of model to the other housemothers she hoped to introduce to the Community.

Here then an attempt was made to give these damaged boys the primary provision they had lacked. It is difficult to describe in cold words how this is done, as it is so much a matter of feeling, of the readiness to give oneself, of atmosphere, of all-embracing concern and care. The boys were not, for example, got up in the morning in the ordinary sense of that term, but were gently, gradually but very firmly coaxed out of bed. Rising to face another day, and at the end of it surrendering oneself to unconsciousness, are perhaps the most difficult parts of the daily routine for an unintegrated child. It is not a case of being lazy or uncooperative and needing to be coerced; it is a matter of simply finding it incredibly difficult, and having to be helped over the recurring hurdle, morning and evening. Bedtime is crucial. Hot-water bottles are filled for each boy, by the staff, and they are coaxed into bed, though after a while coaxing becomes less necessary because they have learned from experience that once in bed they are the object of further attention – tucking up, a good-night kiss, perhaps cuddling, perhaps some-

---

*Even if we can accept all that this boy says, it does not necessarily follow that he was incarcerated the whole time in 'number one'. He might well have spent his days in school or the trade-training department, returning to separation in the evenings.

thing to suck. One hears a sixteen year old saying quite unashamedly that he hasn't had his cuddle yet, and being, quite manifestly, an infant. These boys alone at that time had breakfast in their own 'home' with attention paid to individual fads and whims, instead of going over to the central dining-room. Their tantrums were tolerated in the sense that they were not regarded as offences, but were nevertheless held firmly in check so that a boy could hurt neither himself nor anyone else. The housefather was 'Mr Mac', Pat Drew was simply 'Pat', and their colleagues were known invariably by their Christian names. When the boys behaved in an infantile way the staff responded – so far as feasible with big boys – as they would to an infant, checking him kindly, patiently, tolerantly, but with unequivocal firmness. Staff doing this kind of work have to recognize with clarity the difference – and it is a crucially important difference – between patient, planned toleration on the one hand, and easy-going, indulgent permissiveness on the other. It is fatally easy too for a worker to 'infantilize' a boy to satisfy his (or her) own needs, and this too has to be guarded against. The superficial, casual observer, seeing these highly skilled people at work, may be unaware of the distinctions. But they are there, and the worker is always conscious of them. If he is not, he is wasting his time and may be doing more harm than good.

There was a different attitude, a different approach to every boy, according to his needs and his personality. He was made to feel that he mattered to someone, and that he was being personally and individually cared for. The loving care he now experienced was something he had never had, and provided a secure refuge from which he could look upon the frightening and hostile world with less fear, and begin to establish himself as a person. Here at last was an opportunity for the growth of satisfying relationships with other people. From this point a boy would begin to look at the men in his environment and see that male strength and aggression could be used to protect and care for others. It is this lack of concern that makes the delinquent.

By early summer 1968 these changes had been or were in the process of being made, and we may well feel that all this constituted a considerable achievement. The principal did not think that, because he was too deeply conscious of what there was still to do, and of course he had at this time no means of knowing whether the small pockets of therapeutic care so far established would be able to survive; whether the adults in the Community would be able to establish sufficient real control (as distinct from the superficial control of 'discipline') to mitigate the aggression and destructiveness being displayed by the boys, which sometimes reached terrifying proportions. He was also, with very good reason, conscious of the reservations of some of the staff and the hostility of others, directed not only at himself but also at those of his colleagues who had presumed to assert their loyalty to the new ways. Notably these were the chaplain (The Rev. W. G. M. Douglas) and Trevor Blewett, and it was heartening to have their support. The satisfaction it gave however was somewhat diminished by the thought of the cost at which it was given. To Bill Douglas hostility was expressed in open threats and jeers. He is a bachelor, but Trevor Blewett has a wife and young family who were now subjected to the same ostracism, the same wounding remarks, as the principal's family, while he himself was regarded by many simply as a traitor.

Some men would have given up – would indeed have convinced themselves that it was their duty to wife and children to do so – which Balbernie came very near to doing. He recalls this period as one of almost unabated distress and doubt, alleviated only by the support of his wife (who freely confesses that her loyalty was much strained at times), the allegiance of a tiny proportion of the staff – and of course the unequivocal championship of the Rainer Foundation.

It was at this point that the Rainer Foundation decided to withdraw – to surrender to the Home Office their certificate of approval. To Balbernie this seemed to imply closure, and while in time it was revealed that the catastrophe was not quite as overwhelming as that, the letter he now received from the Foundation's Chairman heralded a period – still not terminated – of agonizing doubt about the Community's future, a burden added to all the stress, unhappiness and uncertainty in which his daily life was lived.

# 4 Complications

The Rainer Foundation started life about a century ago as the Police Court Mission of the Church of England Temperance Society, out of whose work grew the present probation service. When probation became a state service the Mission looked round for other useful fields of service, taking a new lease of life and a new name. Among other things the new foundation started in 1940 the Cotswold Approved School.

In 1968 the committee and officers of the Foundation read the White Paper *Children in Trouble*, which gave a preview of probable future legislation in the field of juvenile delinquency. This paper revealed the government's intention of abolishing the approved-school order and the approved-school service as we had hitherto known it. Instead, children of the kind that had formerly been committed to approved schools would in future be placed in the care of the local children's officer who would have the duty of finding suitable placements for them, just as he already did for children taken into care for other reasons. With this end in view a system of 'community homes' was to be organized, beginning of course with adaptation of existing homes, including approved schools. Control, broadly speaking, would be in the hands of the children's departments of local authorities, acting singly or in consortium, who would have the duty of providing a range of homes adapted to the varying needs of different kinds of children. It appeared to the Rainer Foundation that their position *vis-à-vis* the Cotswold Community would be very difficult, if not impossible. Either effective control would pass to a local authority, in which case there would be little opportunity for the Foundation to fulfil any useful function; or, if they wished to preserve their independence, they would have to find much more money than was practicable for a voluntary society. Equally important however was another section of the White Paper. This proposed various other ways of helping children who displayed behaviour difficulties, but for whom residential provision was not necessary, and these it called 'intermediate treatment'. This was very much the Rainer Foundation's concern, for it had already done and was doing much distinguished work in this field, of which the best known is perhaps the Hafod Meurig Adventure Centre in Wales. This is a short-term residential establishment mainly for boys on probation, on the lines of the well-known Outward Bound centres, where boys can learn to be 'tough' in an accept-able way in such things as mountaineering, climbing, sailing and orienteering. It was clear to them that if the White Paper proposals became law, they would on the one hand be in a very difficult position with regard to the Cotswold, while on the other there would be tremendously increased scope for them in the field of intermediate treatment. They therefore wrote to the Home Office – though not without a great deal of heart-burning – in June 1968 to the effect that they proposed to surrender their certificate of approval. They expressed their deep regret that this action had become necessary, particularly in view of the success already achieved by Mr Balbernie, and their conviction that given time and resources they would have reached their goal.

One deeply sympathizes with the Rainer Foundation in its dilemma, though without knowledge of the background their action might seem somewhat precipitate, because the White Paper's proposals had not at that stage even been incorporated in a Bill, much less enacted; indeed they were not enacted until over a year later. This is how it appeared to me until I had the opportunity of discussing the matter with the Foundation's chairman, Mr J. H. Emlyn Jones, and its secretary, Mr R. C. Howell. From this discussion it emerged that the Foundation was in sufficiently close touch with the Home Office to know that the probability of the proposals being enacted was very great indeed, and it would have been irresponsible simply to sit back and wait to see what happened. So, far from being hasty, their action now appears as a carefully considered appraisal of the situation as it would be in a year or so, and a very reasonable advance decision on the necessary action when that situation should emerge. It was clearly much sounder policy to foresee impending difficulties before they emerged, so that there was time to plan for them, rather than being forced to rush into ill-considered action when the difficulties were already upon them.

The Home Office was unable to disagree with the Foundation's reading of the White Paper, and discussions were entered into with the children's department about possible ways of continuing the work, which meant in effect finding someone else to take over the certificate when the Foundation surrendered it. Those discussions were already in hand when Mr Emlyn Jones came down to the Cotswold to convey to the staff the Foundation's decision. This very unpleasant task he courageously undertook not only because a very long and happy association was to be severed, but also because – and this fact cannot be blinked at – if some other body could not be found to take over the Community, its staff would all be out of a job.

It was nevertheless a staggering blow to all concerned, because the Rainer Foundation after all had initiated the conversion, understood and sympathized with what was going on, and had staunchly supported the principal in what he was doing. Who was to know whether their successors – even supposing they could be found – would be equally sympathetic? That they should be equally enthusiastic was too much to hope for.

One might have forgiven Balbernie if at this stage he had entertained the hope that no successor could be found. He could then have said, 'Thank God for that. Now I can abandon this thankless task with an easy conscience, get my wife and family away from this frightening environment, and sleep peacefully at night.' He did no such thing. He was appalled and nonplussed, but he joined with vigour in the search that was being made for the means of continuing the work under some other *aegis*. Fortunately neither he nor the Foundation was without support. The Home Office naturally did not want to see the experiment cut short before it had got into its stride, and Derek Morrell, who was then head of the Home Office Children's Department, displayed a personal commitment to the venture and all that it stood for that is rare in a civil servant. Means must be found, means would be found, he said, to keep things going. He said this not only to the Foundation and to Balbernie, but to the whole staff. Publicly and unequivocally – indeed enthusiastically

– he identified himself with what was being done at the Cotswold and expressed his absolute conviction that it would continue. With backing of this kind Balbernie was able to assure the staff that the experiment would not be prematurely ended, in spite of what their employers had told them, and then returned to the problem of trying to find the means to justify that statement.

Either of two courses seemed possible. Approaches might be made to some of the large charitable foundations, asking them to provide the capital with which to establish a 'Cotswold-Community Trust' that might then take over the property and administer the Community – as the Rainer Foundation had done – as a 'voluntary' approved school. This however would merely postpone for a year or two consideration of the problem which had brought about the present *impasse*. The Foundation were of course more than eager to see their work continued, and Morrell explained to Balbernie, as he had explained to the Foundation, that although the establishment of a genuine therapeutic community within the approved-school system was a project dear to his heart, he was also anxious to demonstrate – if possible – that the kind of conversion they were engaged in was practicable within the confines of official governmental administration. Provision for the residential treatment of 'delinquent' children was soon to be a local-government responsibility and here was a chance to test the feasibility of locating a therapeutic unit within the local-authority framework. Indeed the arrangements envisaged in the proposed Act would seem to make any other arrangement impossible.

This was the second possible approach, which was in fact decided upon, and difficult, complex negotiations were entered into, principally between the Foundation and the Wiltshire County Council, but with the Home Office also in the picture. The outcome was a most unusual compromise, temporary in nature, but at least securing the experiment for another couple of years. The County Council were favourably disposed to the idea of taking over the Community, but not yet. This is not surprising as they could not be expected to buy a pig in a poke, and they would have to find a considerable capital sum. The Rainer Foundation naturally wanted to realize on their property in order to use the proceeds on their new work in the sphere of intermediate treatment, but were willing to wait a couple of years. On the other hand their present work and new commitments were occupying much of their time and energy, and they were unable to continue any longer responsibility for the day-to-day management of the Community, though they would be happy in the interim period to continue financial responsibility. The Foundation's Cotswold School Committee was therefore disbanded, and its management functions taken over by the County Council. The singular situation thus came into being in which one body – the County Council – was responsible for running the place, while another, the Foundation, owned it and retained financial responsibility. Balbernie therefore found himself with three masters – the Foundation, the County Council and the Home Office, which issues the regulations under which approved schools are administered, and is responsible for seeing that those regulations are observed.

The complexities generated by this arrangement in the day-to-day running of the place – getting consent for this or that alteration or adaptation from one master (or two) and then getting financial approval from another (or others), and the planning of the future, even just the immediate future – are better imagined than described, and not easily imagined, though to be sure it gave the principal – as the officers of the Foundation pointed out to me – unprecedented scope for playing off one master against the others! This situation was further exacerbated by a serious financial problem. When the new regime began it had been expected that over the first three years a sum of £100,000 would be found for the rebuilding and refurbishing of premises and equipment. It was not of course to be provided by the Foundation which, as a voluntary charitable body, could hardly deploy funds of that order. They were however to have raised a loan, with Home Office backing, but in the new circumstances this was hardly feasible. The bursar therefore now had to try somehow to finance the changes from ordinary revenue – a difficult proposition because at the Cotswold, as at any establishment financed partly from public funds, budgeting has to be done a long time before the money is expected to be spent. Balbernie arrived in September 1967 in the middle of a financial year, and obviously no substantial changes involving money were possible that year. But estimates had already been submitted and approved for the following year, ending March 1969 – eighteen months ahead! The Home Office and the Foundation were as helpful as they could possibly be, and allowed the switching of money from one account to another in a way that must have horrified some of the official accountants. The fact remained, however, that finances had been settled and arranged for the eighteen months following the changeover on the same basis as hitherto, making no allowance for the upheavals of the conversion to a therapeutic community. Briefly then, in spite of the ingenuity of Bill Douglas (who was in the business side of industry before he became a parson), and the helpful attitude of the Home Office, money was very short indeed.

Coupled with the financial stringency, so unwieldy and cumbersome an administrative machine was bound to be a perpetual source of frustration and irritation, but burdensome though it was, it was not considered too high a price to pay for the continuance of the work. The question continuously niggling away at the back of Balbernie's mind was this – *would* this arrangement enable the work to continue, or would it in the end kill it? This is a question that calls for careful examination, as others may in the future find themselves in a position not wholly dissimilar, and it raises the whole problem of the viability of specialized experimental work under local government.

Of Balbernie's three masters he could feel completely confident in the future of the understanding and support of only one, the Children's Department of the Home Office, because of the rather unconventional personal commitment of Morrell. Confident though he was of that support, it must be remembered that the Home Office has little if any direct control over what goes on in an approved school or community home. Its function is restricted to seeing that the law and regulations derived from that law are carried out, and *advising* on the best means of doing so. They can inspect and visit the schools, and can give advice and encouragement (or, in suitable circumstances, discouragement) informally to the head, but their formal approaches must be through the managers of the school, in this case the local authority. So long as there is no breach of law or regulations the managers can if they so wish completely ignore advice offered by the Home Office.

It is important at this point to remind ourselves exactly what it was that the people at the Cotswold were doing. They were not merely running an approved school. That in itself would have been difficult enough because there was much uncertainty and confusion as to exactly what it was that the approved schools were supposed to be doing. Not everyone by any means – not even all the magistrates who sent children there – completely realized that the schools had no longer any punitive function, and one has heard justices, making an approved-school order, assume a very minatory 'This will teach you a lesson' tone of voice. There was considerable difference of opinion among magistrates, among laymen and perhaps most of all among approved-school staffs about how the schools' function of 'the readjustment and social re-education of the child' * was best carried out – whether by discipline and training, whether by ordinary boarding-school education, or by methods based on a therapeutic approach – or all three in combination. But the Cotswold Community was not even engaged in this uncertain task; it was engaged in the highly specialized, very complex, skilled and difficult task of converting a very orthodox approved school into a therapeutic community. This naturally involves a total commitment to an approach that is fully understood by few, and is by no means generally accepted as a valid approach to the problems of delinquency. If they were to be successful in their task (which, as it was experimental, might well have different results from those hoped for) they must be free to carry out that task in a way that allowed them to use their skills and expertise. This includes finding and employing people who have the skills and expertise, and training those who do not, and using methods which might to the uninformed seem highly questionable. The Home Office was broadly in sympathy with that approach but was not in a position to enforce its views. The Rainer Foundation was equally committed but was in the process of withdrawing. This left, of Balbernie's three 'masters', the local authority – the County Council. The depart-

* *Eighth Report of the Children's Department*, 1961, HMSO.

ment of the Council directly responsible was the Children's Department, hitherto not without experience of approved-school work but, like any other children's department, entirely without experience in the conduct of a therapeutic community. Balbernie's contact there was of course the Children's Officer, and here appeared a glimmer of light. Ted Brown proved to be a man of considerable stature, highly respected by his colleagues and his committee. A man moreover who spoke much the same language as Balbernie, and to whom he could readily make himself understood. In spite of the many other duties that claimed his time and interest, he threw himself straightaway with great ardour into the project, to the great comfort and encouragement of the people at the Community. It must be borne in mind, however, that no matter how great Brown's influence may have been with his committee, the fact remains that, like any other administrative officer, he is the servant of the committee. His committee (I speak of children's committees in general), however well intentioned, consists largely of councillors who find themselves there for all the diverse, complex, sometimes highly personal and irrelevant reasons that people do get on to councils and thence to committees; plus a few coopted members who have been brought in because of their known interest in or experience with children. Even the children's committee, furthermore, is not an autonomous body. It is simply a committee of the County Council to which it is answerable and to which it reports – a body where many large issues are discussed and decided, and to whom such a thing as the Cotswold Community is merely a minor concern of one of its committees. To the Council other committees too bring their reports and requests and demands, and every councillor is eager to grind the no doubt excellent and praiseworthy axe of his own committee. Among all this important and far-reaching business with its relentless competition for funds, the Community – itself merely an adopted child of one of the committees – is bound to be very small fry indeed, and if its interests should happen to clash with those of another committee or project of the Council, no very strong or authoritative voice is likely to be raised on its behalf. It will thus be seen that the ultimate control of the Community is in the power of a body with a multiplicity of interests, which is not only remote and difficult of access, but is unfamiliar with the Community's particular problems, without specialized knowledge of what it is trying to do, only marginally interested in its work, and only faintly identified with the need to make the conversion a success.

None of the foregoing is intended to be disparaging of the Wiltshire County Council or of any of its officers. That Council rescued the Community from possible dissolution and has entered whole-heartedly into its new responsibility. It is simply a description of the position of any experimental, highly specialized piece of work that has been taken over – perhaps reluctantly – by any large local authority. The dangers and uncertainties one sees for the Cotswold Community are absolutely inherent in the situation and are not in any sense the fault of the authority. It was presumably because Morrell was aware of all these pitfalls and difficulties that he was so concerned to 'test the feasibility' of such a situation; if they had not been there no such test would have been necessary. The position of such a piece of work might be different and less hazardous when the regional planning areas envisaged in the 1969 Act come into being – but that remains to be seen. It will also be different and, one fears, more hazardous when, under the recent Social Services Act, children's departments become part of the new social-services department – a process which has already begun.

So it is possible to forgive the people at the Cotswold if they feel they are rather 'out on a limb', and this applies particularly to the principal. Residential work is highly demanding, and people responsibly engaged in it very much need someone – preferably a group of people – upon whom they can 'lean', the need for this support being all the greater when the work is of a highly novel, experimental nature. I am not suggesting that the principal needs the kind of father figure which Balbernie so rightly refuses to be for his staff. Awareness of the kind of need I have in mind arises not in dependent, inadequate people but (and perhaps only) in people who are strong, capable and well integrated, but who have sensitivity, insight and modesty enough to realize that they are not the repository of all wisdom and knowledge, that they cannot alone find the solution to every problem, whether that problem is one concerning the internal affairs of the establishment or one concerning its external relations. The head of such an establishment needs to be able to discuss his problems with people who are intimately familiar with them, and who can each give advice and counsel (or even simply support and encouragement) from the standpoint of his or her own learning and experience in one of the disciplines involved – education, psychiatry, child care, finance and administration, law and penology, psychotherapeutics, staff training and so on. That is the kind of body that should and must be responsible for the management of a place like the Cotswold Community, and not on the one hand a local-government committee exercising remote control by laymen nor on the other a committee of local 'gentry', full of good works and intentions, but empty of informed understanding.

It is imperative furthermore that a piece of work like that being carried on at the Cotswold should have its experimental status recognized and allowed for. By this I mean that for a community home that is engaged in experimental work; that is seeking and trying new ways; that is keeping – as the Cotswold is keeping – an ongoing record and critical analysis of all that is done; that is engaged too in the training of staff – for such an establishment the recognized norms in things like staff ratios and finance do not apply, and exceptional arrangements need to be made. Unless this is done, it becomes impossible for the specific and characteristic work of the Cotswold to continue, and the opportunity for new learning, new insights is lost. It seems to me that it is not altogether fanciful to see the difference between an experimental and a non-experimental community home as akin to the difference between a teaching hospital and any other hospital. Certainly some such special status is called for, and it would be one of the functions of the kind of management committee I have in mind to secure, to defend and to maintain that special status.

In the meantime Balbernie and his colleagues struggle along with the management that is vouchsafed them, grateful to the Council for survival, believing in what they are doing, and perfectly confident in its successful outcome if only they are allowed to continue to do it.

# 5 The Community Begins to Take Shape

In Chapter 3 we saw the new style of living unit getting under way in Thames House, with a couple of dozen boys, a house-master and housemother, and three group leaders. This was in the nature of a crash programmme for boys who had indeed been in some measure infected by the subculture but had not been at the school so long as to be considered beyond hope of recovery. The staff of Thames, it will be recalled, had for a time regular seminars, though the purpose of this training was rather for its future value than in the expectation that it would radically affect what was then going on in Thames. Nevertheless the new attitude made a real appearance. Regimentation and punishment disappeared and an atmosphere of parental 'caring' began to be manifest. There were housemeetings in which staff and boys together discussed what was going on and considered together ways of dealing with difficulties that arose.

A tangible example of the new approach was to be seen in the matter of hot-water bottles. I single this out, from several possible examples, because it is the one most likely to evoke derisive jeers from the unsympathetic. It was simply made known to the boys that hot-water bottles would henceforward be available at bedtime *but* – and this, to some, will seem just as derisory as the presence of the bottles themselves in an approved school – a boy who asked for one was not merely told to take it. It was filled, carefully dried and personally handed to the boy by the staff member concerned. In this kind of way were boys now given – often for the first time in their lives – the sort of loving personal attention that most of us have enjoyed – and taken for granted – in childhood from our parents.

All this was difficult for the boys to understand and it was soon realized that even their brief contact with the old sub-culture had deeply affected them and they were inclined either to be suspicious of all this or to regard it with contempt. Never-theless, while it is doubtful how many of the 'leftovers' from the old days were positively helped, there is no doubt whatever that new boys entering Thames House were subjected to a totally different experience from that of new boys arriving earlier. One boy told me very graphically about his introduction to Thames, which must have been towards the end of the Thames experiment. He had been over to the stores to collect his kit on his first day, and on returning to the house began to go upstairs with it. Looking up, he saw two boys appear at the top of the stairs and begin to descend – 'Proper hard cases they were – leather jackets and all that.' He knew exactly what to expect. There is an underground grapevine which in some mysterious way seems to transmit across the boundaries of individual institutions the mores and practices of approved-school life. He was sure that unless he scuttled down again quickly to make way for the two young lords above there would be drastic consequences for him, and probably, as he was a new boy, he would suffer those consequences anyway. He confesses to having been 'scared out of his wits', but before he had time to reverse direction and get out of their way, 'Do you know what they did, Mr Wills? They went back up and said, "Come on up, new kid." I was still scared – didn't know what might happen when I got up there. But it was all right. I went on up and they just smiled at me and then went down themselves.'

So even during the Thames House era, which only lasted about a year, a new and much more civilized atmosphere had begun to make itself felt; for there is very little doubt that twelve months earlier that boy would have been beaten up – if not at that moment, then later, outside, perhaps under a duffle coat, or suffered a far worse and terrifying initiation. In a paper given to the Approved Schools Conference in 1967 Christopher Beedel said, 'Ultimately young people can only confirm the care they have received by becoming able, in however limited a way, to care for others.' This episode I have recounted from the Community's first year or so is not as trifling as it may seem. To me it is evidence of a drastic change from the habit of thought that assumes the necessity to terrorize a newcomer, to a new, quite different, civilized mode of thought that assumes the need to care for him. In a small way those two 'hard' boys coming downstairs were in Beedel's words confirming the care they had received from the staff of the Community; were in themselves justification for the changes now being brought about.

Thames House, however, was but one part of the work, and while it was being watched hopefully and anxiously, it was necessary to keep the rest of the Community in operation and, so far as possible, moving towards its goal. We saw in Chapter 3 how the grossly immature boys, the least integrated, were gradually being collected together in one group and housed in a building that came to be called the Cottage, with a new and well-trained housemaster and housemother. At the same time two other houses – those on either side of the square – were drastically reduced in numbers in the hope of facilitating the beginning of the new approach. The central house in the square – George's – became in effect a repository for the remainder of the boys. It was manifestly impossible to inaugurate the new order everywhere at once, even in the tentative way that was then being attempted, because even if all the staff were sympathetic – which many of them were not – they still needed to be trained. George's therefore continued to house some two dozen boys, and the staff were thought of as carrying out something in the nature of a holding operation; in Richard Balbernie's words, they 'kept things stuck together with sticky tape and sealing wax', while change was being effected elsewhere.

Change there certainly was, because in addition to much chopping and changing of boys and staff from house to house in the interest of reorganization, or to cope with emerging crises, there was also much coming and going of staff. Twenty-one men had been asked to leave by the end of 1968, in addition to those who had left of their own volition, though it must be remembered that fifty had left in the two years preceding the changeover. These were the people professionally concerned directly with the boys – teachers, instructors, housemasters. The same flux was not evident among staff less directly concerned – cleaners, cooks, craftsmen, night-watchmen. These were in a sense above the battle because penological techniques were not their business; they were not involved in 'controlling' the boys, were not identified with the hierarchy of command. For this reason communication between them and the new principal was easy, and for the same reason there had been some real communication, at a matter-of-fact, informal level between them and the boys. To some with a natural gift for empathy – particularly perhaps to night-watchman Bill Sampson – boys had felt able to reveal their inmost fears and anxieties. It was one of the aims of the new regime to make much greater use of these natural gifts, because boys in an approved school are just as likely (in some schools alas more likely) to make relationships with them as with those whose professional function it is.

These people then were outside the dispute, but the others from the beginning of the year were firmly arrayed in two camps, the small but growing beleaguered group who were for the change, and the large but diminishing group who were not only against it, but bitterly opposed to it. The 'for' group contained a few older men from the old regime, some of whom are still there and still enthusiastic supporters of the new regime. During this period they had a difficult time at the hands of their colleagues, who accused them of being stooges and traitors. But in the main they were senior men who had been there long enough, and had status enough, to be able to withstand these attacks not, it is true, without discomfort, but without feeling totally destroyed. They were moreover in the main married men with homes to return to when the day's work was over. The people who really suffered were the young, single men and especially those who were concerned with child care, the house staff. It is true that the 'for' group gradually increased in size and stature as malcontents left and new men came to replace them, but this was a slow process, and the 'antis' were numerous as well as senior. The child-care staff, the housemasters, had hitherto been accorded the lowest status of all (excluding house-mothers, but they were so few that for all practical purposes they were ignored) and one of the reforms that was integral to the idea of a therapeutic community was their upgrading in the general esteem.

If it is to be properly carried out, the function of the child-care staff (sometimes called parenting) calls for gifts, qualities, skills, expertise and training quite as great as those of any of their colleagues. There had been three main degrees of status among the staff, with an internal pecking order in each. Teachers were the highest grade, instructors were close behind them, and a long, derisory distance below them were housemasters and housemothers. The residential child-care worker, however – especially when, as in this case, he is dealing with severely disturbed and deprived children – needs to have personal qualities of sensitivity, empathy, intuitive understanding, stability and integrity. He needs to have some understanding of the way the human being develops from infancy to adulthood, in body, mind and feeling, and the various ways in which this development can be stunted and warped. He must know something of how people react to one another in a group, and how to perceive, anticipate and handle group feelings and tendencies. He must have enough personal awareness and insight to recognize what effects the group and the individuals in it are having upon himself, and see that his judgement is not clouded nor his competence impaired by those effects. He needs to have the kind of personal authority that makes people feel safe in his presence rather than the kind that intimidates and overawes. He needs to know something about voluntary and statutory social-work agencies and how to make use of their services. All this is very far from the old conception (which is dying very hard) of the residential child-care worker as a low-grade unskilled childminder, who in the past, it has to be admitted, did not always have this kind of stature, and even those who did enjoyed very little professional status. At any rate they had enjoyed very little at the Cotswold School up to 1968, and still enjoyed little in the eyes of those who were resistant to the change. So difficult did it prove in the early days to endow them with the esteem and status to which they were entitled that it was necessary for a time to pander to the old culture by putting teachers – because of the superior status accorded them by the boys as well as staff – in charge of houses.

One of the young house staff has told me something of what he and his young colleagues endured during that difficult year. The new young men were distributed among the houses, sometimes with sympathetic, sometimes with less sympathetic colleagues. They attempted to keep the routine going by their personal authority, by the relationships (if any) they were able to establish with the boys, by persuasion and exhortation, by anything except punishment and the threat of punishment. They were like new wine in old bottles, or perhaps more properly like new parts that had been fitted to an old machine in the effort to make that machine do something quite different from what it had been created for. In time the machinery would be changed or completely adapted to its new purpose but in the meantime life was almost intolerable for these 'new parts'. The boys were in any case inclined to be a little contemptuous of them because they were 'only' housemasters. As they were accustomed to a punitive culture, whether one thinks of the formal one or the subculture, they naturally regarded non-punishing adults as weak and incompetent, and led them a fearful dance. They would begin the day by refusing to get out of bed.* When he was finally extricated from his blankets a boy would wait until the housemaster went to another room to deal with a similar situation, then get back into bed, and that was the kind of pattern all day, until the early hours of the morning when the housemaster, coming repeatedly from his own bed to quell a disturbance, would find everyone in bed, blankets pulled over faces and beds shaking from suppressed – or unsuppressed – giggles. To many of the old hands all this was clear evidence of the folly and uselessness of the new approach, and whether or not there was *conscious* collusion between the boys and the 'anti' staff, there is no doubt that the boys were aware that the distress they brought to some members of the staff brought satisfaction to others. They did everything they could to break the integrity of the new approach, and the concern, patience and strength of the new men. During this period scores of windows were broken, locks smashed, stores broken into. Boys would climb onto roofs and defy the staff to do anything about it. One boy indeed sat on a roof with a bottle of barbiturates which he had acquired by breaking into the medical room, and

* I am writing here of the situation as it was in the early days, with young inexperienced men working sometimes alongside unsympathetic colleagues, among the 'normal' population of the Community. The position in the Cottage (Chapter 3), where a highly skilled, trained and united *team* were dealing with a small group of grossly disturbed boys, is not to be taken as inconsistent with the above.

threatened suicide. This is not to say that the whole regime had broken down and descended into total chaos. That was never the case. The daily routine was, with difficulty, maintained; in the main boys were got to where they should be at about the time they were supposed to be there; there was never total collapse. But in so far as this much was achieved, it was achieved at great personal cost to the staff. Every day, in every house, the boys continued their pressure at every point to make life as difficult as possible in all the thousand and one ways that boys accustomed to being controlled by an imposed discipline can use to make intolerable the life of those who decline to control them in this particular way. There were childish practical jokes, deceptions, leg-pulls, bland ignorance of the answer to simple questions – all that kind of thing, with continual minor infractions and minor disorders. That was the general pattern, but in addition to these daily trials and pressures few days would pass without some major destructive delinquency such as breaking-in, beating up another boy, climbing on roofs or window smashing, by small groups of boys in one house or another.

As if all this was not enough, the distress of the new young house-staff was exacerbated by a daily ordeal in the staff dining-room. Here, as in most disciplined establishments of the kind, the staff seated themselves in due order of rank and precedence. A group of the older men who resented the changes – and to whom indeed, it must in fairness be said, it seemed that their school was simply being ruined by a set of cranks – always sat together. Throughout the meal snide remarks, oblique references to the latest delinquency committed by the boys, sarcastic suggestions about the next probable reform, were bandied about with knowing smiles and sometimes outright laughter. None, of course, addressed to the young men, but all aimed at them, and just loud enough for them to hear. These attacks were made from a position of strength by men who were in the main older, senior in years of service, of senior rank at least in their own estimation, and who much outnumbered those they attacked. The exigencies of duty hours and rosters were such that often a young man would have to face this without the support of like-minded colleagues who were eating elsewhere or at another time, and there was never anything to be done but just suffer it all in silence. Even the deepest conviction of the rightness of one's cause serves little to make this kind of thing more endurable, and it is a great tribute to the courage and confidence of those young men, and to their faith in what they were doing, that they survived this terrible period and are – some of them – still there to see and enjoy the order that has grown out of the disorder of those days. It is order of a totally different kind from that which preceded that painful year; an order based on mutual respect, on caring relationships, on good parenting.

By the time Thames House had been in operation twelve months or so all the boys remaining from the old regime had gone, and another house outside the square had been made available. By the spring of 1970 – as we shall see – the whole of the square was being used for other purposes and the boys were distributed among four houses well outside it. They were : the Cottage (at which we looked briefly in Chapter 3) which was once the lock-up or Quiet Room; Number Eleven as it was now called, which had once been the pre-release house and subsequently Thames; the Rookery, converted staff houses about halfway down the main drive; and Orchard Flats, which as its name implies is in the orchard and was once staff flats. The average occupancy of these four units in the spring of 1970 was about thirteen, the Cottage being below that average and the Orchard above it. By now the shape of things to come was clearly to be seen, though the number of boys was still rather small for the administrative set-up, and at least one more living unit was envisaged.

Looking back on those days when the process of change was producing its maximum impact in disaffection and disorder, Richard Balbernie says it is now possible to see a clear watershed, a distinct dividing of the ways. It appeared when the Rookery was established in what had been staff houses halfway down the drive. To him, however it may have seemed to others, the effect of all the boys having been concentrated in houses round the back square (which also used to be known as 'the boys' square') was to give the impression of their being hemmed in or surrounded. Into this area of concentration the staff came every morning as from the outside; as from, it almost seemed, the besieging forces. Now, the boys (or at least some of them) were living 'outside' and walked in each morning to come to work. He says it seems naïve, but a real change seems to date from that time.

The present stage was reached only after enormous difficulty, surmounted by determination and faith as enormous. Not only did most of the old staff find the new circumstances intolerable and move on (either voluntarily or with a little encouragement), but it was by no means always tolerable, during the period of greatest change, even to new staff, quite apart from the opposition to which I have referred. Men would come along full of enthusiasm for the idea of a therapeutic community – sometimes straight from training courses – men who might well indeed have worked happily and successfully in such a community once it was established, only to find that the tensions and stresses involved in the operation of creating that therapeutic environment, and creating it out of an institution that had been quite differently oriented, was more than they could cope with. Even apart from that problem, however, was the further one that not everyone has the integrity of personality or the strength of character necessary to exercise responsibility in the way that men are expected to exercise it at the Cotswold – one that calls upon them to rely on themselves, to exercise personal authority and not rely on a structure or an hierarchy of control. Trevor Blewett, the head of group living, has seen the emergence of a regular pattern of response from new staff members as they settle – or fail to settle! – in. First there is the honeymoon period of dewy-eyed idealism, when the new man, full of enthusiasm, tends to expect everything to work perfectly and all his colleagues – since they have chosen to come and work at such places – to be paragons of virtue. He sees himself as about to be involved in a number of ideal relationships with the boys. They will naturally like him because his intentions are so honourable, and he is unaware (except perhaps in a purely theoretical way) that he is just as likely to evoke negative as positive transferences; that is to say, the boys are just as likely to transfer to him negative feelings they had for a parent, as any positive feelings they may have had. (The grossly deprived boys will have nothing to transfer!) The new man now begins to discover that his colleagues are merely human after all and that there are faults even in the Cotswold Community. Then he is further discouraged by finding that the boys do not immediately respond to his friendly approaches but test him out in a variety of ways, even that some of them seem positively to dislike him. In spite of his enlightened and 'caring' attitude, they still behave like delinquents, and he finds that he is expected, without temper and without resentment, to 'confront' them with their delinquent conduct, not just gloss over it; and he is expected to do that himself, with boys with whom he is trying to build a 'good relationship'. All this makes him feel very exposed and vulnerable, and he tries to find someone who might perhaps save his feelings, who might take some of that responsibility off his shoulders, someone in short who will be a good parent to him. But that is the pattern of the hierarchical structure, and the function of the senior staff at the Cotswold is, in effect, to 'fail' in the role of parent-figure to the staff. A man is not going to be much use as a centre of authority within his group if he is dependent upon someone outside it. It is a central principle at the Community that while there must be the fullest cooperation and mutual understanding among staff, with every kind of advice and consultancy, in his dealings with the boys a man must rely on his own resources and on that web of feeling and shared experience that we call 'a relationship', and on nothing else. Only so will he present to the boys a figure of personal authority and integrity instead of a mere lay figure, and only a man who can stand steadfast and rock-like in his own two shoes is really cut out for the kind of work that is done at the Cotswold Community. This is the point at which the new man makes the adjustment – or not. It is fully understood at the Cotswold that he is not likely to make that adjustment, and indeed will feel badly let down, unless someone gets him to see exactly what is happening to him, and how the attempt to provide himself with a parent-figure is no solution to that problem with which he is faced. If he can see this, and is a big enough man to act accordingly, he will survive; if not, he will move on.

All this may seem rather hard on the new man but – to me at least – it seems perfectly sound. One of the interesting phenomena of our time in the field of the treatment of delinquent and maladjusted young people – or for that matter in the field of education generally – has been the growth here and there of experimental or unorthodox institutions, under the guidance and control of a man who is assumed to be a person of exceptional ability. The criticism that is levelled at such places is that their success is not dependent upon a method or technique, but upon the special gifts of a particular man – 'And what happens when so and so goes?' There has been, as I now reluctantly see, some justice in this criticism, but the trouble has been not necessarily that the head was an irreplaceable genius, but rather that he insisted on being a controlling father-figure. His tendency to assume all responsibility created a tendency also to prevent his colleagues growing to his stature if they stayed with him. This mistake the Cotswold Community is determined to avoid by dispersing responsibility widely among the staff. But that is not all. The experimental schools to which I have referred have tended to be successful – so far as they *have* been successful – because they have been relatively small and each head has been able to stamp his personality on his own school. It has often been assumed by onlookers that the idiosyncrasies of that personality are the specific virtues of the school, and that when that personality goes the virtues of the school have gone. I am far from sure whether this is an assumption that is justified, but even if it is, and certainly in so far as it is, then the particular genius of the Cotswold Community is that it is making the opportunity for the creation of several such small and idiosyncratic units, each under the control of a head who is able to stamp his personality upon it but which – as it is an integral part of a larger whole – will not 'die' when that man moves on, but will merely adapt itself to the idiosyncracies of his successor, and will be supported by the rest of the community while the change is taking place.

It will be seen therefore that the people in charge of a living unit have to all intents and purposes not only the function of temporary parents, but are also heads each of his own small child-care establishment. They, and not, as in so many establishments, senior colleagues, have contact with parents, with social workers, with prospective employers, as well as with other educators and social workers within the Community. Each unit now has its own premises, its own backyard and boundaries, its own style of living, though in respect of the last named it has to be said that they have not yet entirely shaken off the old imposed pattern of total community – meals are still taken in a central dining-room. Even in this sphere, however, there is movement. Not every meal is taken in the common dining-room, and it is hoped that in the fullness of time each unit will eat 'at home', except perhaps for the midday meal. After all, this would merely be repeating the pattern of normal life, where it is customary to leave home in the morning and return in the evening.

Not that this is by any means the universal practice at the Cotswold. The boys at the Cottage, as will be recalled, are of a very immature, unintegrated kind who are still seeking the primary experience of a secure enveloping mother which they missed in infancy. These boys are encouraged – if they wish – to return at frequent intervals to the unit: for elevenses, for afternoon tea-break, or on any excuse or pretext, so long as they need it; and indeed so great is the need of these boys to cling to the home base that it is hoped that some at least of their educational programme may soon be 'at home'. But unintegrated boys are not peculiar to the Cottage – every group contains boys in varying stages of development towards integration (and in varying stages of settling in), and in every unit there is likely to be a boy or two who needs the reassurance of frequent returns to the vicinity of the known and trusted unit staff, and the familiar safe environment of 'home'.

An essential if not indeed vital and central element of the kind of environmental therapy carried out at the Cotswold Community is the concept of identification. We all have in the course of our development a variety of identification figures, some weak, some strong, and most of us can recall people in our youth whom we greatly admired, respected or loved – or all three. With such a person there is likely to be strong identification feelings; consciously or unconsciously we tend to copy his ways, assume his attitudes, admire the things he admires, despise the things he despises. While we often succeed in convincing ourselves that we admire him *because* of this or that attitude or opinion, it is often the case that the admiration or affection for the person comes first, and the admiration for and adoption of his attributes follows. Speaking of what makes people fall in love, Mrs Humphrey Ward makes one of her characters say, 'Propinquity does it', and it is much the same with identification figures. The young person is going to identify anyway – it is his nature to do so. In the old days boys identified with the leaders of the subculture, fearsome and unpleasant though they seemed, and in consequence strove themselves to become the objects of fear, very often with the passage of time replacing the old leaders as they moved on.

The aim of the Community is to provide ample opportunity to identify with someone whose style of life, attitude to life and philosophy of life are such that, to say the least, no harm can come from their adoption by other people. This is not a matter of imposing by a more subtle means than 'discipline' a preconceived pattern of behaviour; it is a matter of trying to ensure that something that is going to take place anyway – identifying with others – is not done in a way that will later bring distress, to the boy concerned, to his relations, his friends, eventually to his wife and children. This is a further reason why workers in a therapeutic community must be people not only of stability and personal authority; they must also be people with sound moral standards and personal integrity, good models in the mature use of masculine aggression certainly, but good models also in all the things that make an upright, honest, caring person. There is no use in such a place for the kind of person who has no scruples about even what are thought of as very minor venalities like falsifying income-tax returns or dodging the conductor on the bus. The worker with delinquent boys must be, in the real sense of the word, admirable. All this makes them sound like paragons of virtue. They do need to be better than average; they must be at least, in Winnicott's phrase, 'good enough'.

Identification commonly takes place where there is affection and admiration and no one is more likely to be an identification object than one who is the object of a positive transference. Here there is a subtle and dangerous trap for the unwary, and one against which the leadership of the Community are constantly warning their colleagues. Delinquent children are very commonly also deprived children. Even those who do not need 'primary provision' do need much highly personalized attention and consideration. They need to be treated with respect in order to enhance their self-respect, they need to be made to feel that they count, that they are important to someone, to be given the dignity and security that arise from the knowledge that someone cares for them. It is in that kind of atmosphere that positive feelings and relationships can arise of the kind that make for identification with the worker. But love, in the sense of tenderness, solicitude, care, provision, is not enough. That the deprived child should have these is right, is indeed essential. But they do not constitute the whole of a caring attitude; especially with the delinquent child, something else is called for. The child must (in Cotswold terminology) be confronted with his delinquency. There is a danger (and I have seen it happening many times) for the worker who is trying to make the kind of provision the deprived child needs, so to identify with him (instead of the reverse) that he glosses over and tries to excuse the delinquent behaviour – in fact colludes with it. This is fatal and is one of the chief failings of many establishments which strive after a loving, therapeutic approach. This is what Balbernie constantly decries as 'woolly permissiveness'. It is no kindness whatever to the child to allow him to suppose for one moment that his dishonesty, his violence, his lack of consideration for others do not matter after all, that it is all due to the way he was brought up or something of that kind, and is not really his fault. The worker is of course aware of the deprivations that have contributed to the growth of a delinquent attitude, and by his caring and provision is trying to compensate for them; but the victim (if indeed that is what he is) must be encouraged to fight against them in the same way as a physically disabled person is encouraged to fight against the consequences of his disability.

In saying this I am not suggesting – nor do the Cotswold people – that he must be punished for his misconduct. What *must* happen is that the very person who has provided all that care and attention must assert strongly, unequivocally, even sometimes aggressively, that delinquent behaviour is wrong and is totally unacceptable. There are many modes of confrontation, some direct, some oblique, some public, some private. It may be done – and sometimes is done – in anger, but it can also be done

calmly and unemotionally, and it can be done with tenderness.
It may be something that happens in a group meeting or something that happens sitting on the edge of a boy's bed at tucking-
up time. It may take the form – publicly or in private – of
interpreting something a boy has said or done, it may be just a
blunt rebuke. The vital thing is that it is done, unfailingly, unequivocally, and preferably by the person with whom the boy
has the strongest relationship. That in itself is evidence of real
care for the child, and must be given with no diminution of the
other kind of care. This is what so many people find difficult.
They cannot rebuke without withholding affection, but this is
what the worker with delinquent children must learn to do.
They are inclined to take an attitude which says in effect, 'Because he is "my" child I must excuse him'; but they need to be
reminded of the well-known theological principle that forgive-
ness is a two-way process and cannot take place without repen-
tance. Their attitude must be one that says in effect, 'In the
matter of your bullying George, nothing can shake my conviction that you have done an evil for which there is no excuse and
for which you should provide redress or reparation; I shall not
be content until you see how evil your conduct was and have
made some effort at redress. But of course my feelings for you,
my care and solicitude for you, will remain unchanged. My love
is also shown in my condemnation of what you have done.'

Unequivocal condemnation of wrong-doing is just as essential
as provision to compensate for deprivation, because if and when
the child identifies with the adult he will 'take into' himself,
among the adults' other attributes and attitudes, something of
his attitude to delinquent behaviour. If the adult is uncertain,
fuzzy, unclear, equivocal in his attitude, the child is going to be
even more so.

This is the dual task of the worker at the Cotswold Community – care and confrontation. To the casual visitor – especially if he is accustomed to normal approved-school discipline
– the care side may seen predominant, with its hot-water
bottles, hot drinks in bed at night, its fussing over little problems, its patient waiting (in the educational programme) until
the child is ready for the next step. These seem to obtrude
because they are unusual and because they are done in the open.

The confrontation – though also done sometimes in the open when the circumstances demand it – is more often done privately. But it is quite clear to the Cotswold staff that unless the confrontation also takes place, the rest is wasted.

Care; confrontation; and I should like to add control, if that were not liable to be misunderstood. In Chapter 2 I made a distinction which is crucial, between men *in* authority and men *of* authority. I spoke of men 'who knew and were able to show that authority is not something that depends upon a system of controls handed down through an hierarchy, but something within a man; something that arises from his own integrity and confidence in himself, and which makes those around him feel safe.' This is the kind of control I am thinking of, and this is the kind of control that is now most successfully being exercised at the Cotswold Community.

I saw, and indeed personally experienced, an example of this kind of authority and control. I was visiting a particular living unit for the first time, and owing to a variety of mishaps I found myself on arrival alone with more than half the boys in the group – eight or ten of them. A curious kind of reciprocal anxiety gradually arose between us. They knew nothing of me except a rumour that I was writing a book, and my presence made them a little uneasy. They expressed this uneasiness by a few questions and much giggling. This made *me* uneasy because in my peculiar role-less state *vis-à-vis* the boys I felt very insecure and vulnerable. It was not for me to assume a role of authority; I was there simply as an observer, and beyond the normal usages of polite intercourse should do no more than observe. This lack of any recognizable attitude increased the anxieties of the boys who began to be a little offensive, making personal remarks with much, almost hysterical, giggling and laughing and whispering. This again increased my own discomfort until I – who have spent a lifetime among such boys – began to feel really anxious myself. I suppose this went on for about half an hour, and I began to feel quite exhausted. Then I heard a distant door slam, and in a moment in walked Fred Green. Fred Green comes to this unit one or two evenings a week as what they call 'continuity resource'; a middle-aged man, tall and well set up, who had served many years under the old regime and was now a loyal, though not slavish, supporter of the new. As he walked in he uttered a cheery greeting of some kind, and immediately all the tension and anxiety – mine as well as theirs – relaxed. They became normal and friendly, I ceased to worry and became more confident. It was not – and this I cannot too strongly emphasize – a matter of suddenly 'behaving' because a master had entered the room and there might be trouble if you didn't. I have seen that far too often not to know the difference. It was a feeling of relief, a return to normality, a sense of *safety*. Here was the new authority really being exercised.

There was another impressive incident in the same category that same evening. I heard a group of boys discussing how another boy had 'got into trouble with Fred Green'. As they seemed to regard this trouble as quite serious I wondered what enormity he had committed and what dire penalty was being inflicted upon him, so I made inquiries. It appears that Micky had said 'Hullo, daddykins' to the father of Susan, the house-mother, when he came to fetch her home. Fred Green happened to hear this and said something like, 'Now then, Micky, don't be stupid to visitors.' That was all. No punishment, no threats, no danger of future consequences. Just a mild rebuke – but a rebuke that counted, and was seriously regarded not only by its recipient but by the onlookers. This is real authority, authority which owes nothing to a system or to 'discipline' or punishment, but arises out of the inner integrity of a man with a real concern for the boys with whom he was working, and who was admired and respected by them. This may seem a trifling incident, and is indeed the kind of thing that is happening all the time, everywhere, at the Cotswold Community; it happens to be one that I personally experienced.

One other thing calls for comment at this stage, rather by way of apology for its non-appearance hitherto than of any detailed discussion of the thing itself. I refer to the Community's relations with the families of the boys. I have not dealt and do not propose to deal at length with this, not because it is not of prime importance in the overall task of the Community, but because my concern is with the actual process of change from an approved school to a therapeutic community, which is largely an internal matter. But I should be doing an injustice to the new regime if I were not to say that they see their work very much as a cooperative effort – the family, the children's department and themselves working together to the end of seeking solutions to the problems that have resulted in the boy's coming to the Community. Rarely does it happen that such a boy is the only member of his family to need help of one kind or another, and rarely does it happen that the members of the family have nothing to contribute to the solution of those problems, whether they are peculiar to the boy or common to the family. There is therefore constant contact, especially between those immediately concerned with a boy, and his family – and by family I mean family, and not merely parents only. Projects are afoot to make this contact more lively and meaningful – such things as weekend or longer visits by the family to the Community, so that they can actually share for a time the life of the Community. These belong largely to the future, but in the meantime there is lively ongoing communication between family and Community, helping each the better to understand the other, and both to a better understanding of the boy.

# 6 Polytechnic

I saw a small mechanical dumper come rattling and banging towards me on one of the Community's internal roads. It was being driven by a young man of my acquaintance whom we shall call Tommy, whose age was thirteen. His whole body expressed ecstasy. He was leaning forward with his head thrown back. The wind ruffled his blond hair, his lips were parted, his grey eyes were shining. As he approached the small triangular island of grass in front of the kitchen building I felt sure that he would go roaring right round it like a fighter pilot doing a victory roll. But he did not. Perhaps he realized that he was observed, for he suddenly straightened himself, squared his shoulders, closed his mouth and assumed the serious demeanour of a man going about his work with a proper sense of dignity, but not without a certain panache permissible to the man with confidence in his own skill. I saw him slap the gear lever into neutral with an elegant follow-through motion, then he treated me to a terminal roar of the engine as he jammed on the brakes and drew up in front of the kitchen door with more of a flourish than I would have thought possible with so ungainly a vehicle. He and his passenger leapt off the dumper and ran into the kitchen, to emerge in a couple of minutes carrying respectively a tray full of mugs and a large teapot. These were firmly stowed and guarded by the passenger, and off they drove with another *accelerando* from the engine. Tea-break for the builders!

The day before, I had spent a couple of hours with Mike Jinks, head of education, while he told me about the philosophy and methods of the Community's education programme, of which he is in charge. Tommy now neatly and charmingly summarized it in that one episode.

In Chapter 2 we were considering the way in which the approved-school boy has often got stuck with a very primitive concept of masculinity. He wants to be a real man, but the only models he has seen of manhood have been crude types who assert themselves by resisting any kind of authority, and use their masculine aggression to domineer over others by means of bullying and a 'hard' façade. This lack of development to proper, positive use of masculinity was to be seen in the cult of the skinhead, with its 'Paki-bashing' and other forms of crude and offensive behaviour. Such boys tend to revolt against the authority of the ordinary day-school, and sometimes resist it so successfully that they emerge from ten years' schooling as innocent of letters and of number (beyond simple counting) as they were on the day they started. Our young dumper driver was not as illiterate as that, but though he was within the normal range of intelligence, he was three or four years retarded in school attainment. He was not yet quite old enough to have been acceptable to the teenage skinhead gangs of his locality, but he had strong leanings in that direction, and had hung around the fringes of any violent or delinquent group he could come across. He had a perfectly proper and laudable desire to be a man, and that was the only kind of manliness he really knew. That was the male image of the culture in which he had been reared. He came to the Cotswold Community.

Exactly what offence was the precipitating cause of his committal is immaterial. He arrived at what he had been told was an approved *school*, and found to his astonishment – and I presume delight – that it was not a school at all; at least it was certainly not a school in his understanding of that word. His idea of school was a place you were made against your will to attend, where a teacher stands in front of you and your peers and tries to force you to do things you do not want to do, to learn things you do not want to learn. If you expressed your feelings about it all you were caned, and when you had been caned a few times you were 'excluded'.* His deeply felt resentment against all this had led him to resist it all, and the older he got the stronger became his resistance. Now he comes to this approved school and is asked, if you please, how he would like to spend his time! He is shown all the possibilities – gardening, pottery and modelling, painting and decorating, joinery, building. He

*I am not putting this forward as every child's conception of school, but only that of a small group, a proportion of whom finish their education in approved schools.

can even work at ordinary school subjects like English or maths, or anything else that takes his fancy such as drama or painting, though very few opt for that kind of thing straight away. These school-haters belong to that very awkward group who could see the end of schooling on the horizon, and when they got into trouble were simply marking time until they could escape the clutches of the schoolmaster for ever. Most of them are quite sure that – given the option – they will never touch a school subject again, but they are mistaken. Young Tommy is in this category, and when he has seen all the possibilities and met the teachers and instructors, he soon knows what he wants to do. A boy who is so eager to demonstrate his masculinity will choose the manliest thing he can find. Engineering is masculine all right, but it involves intricate skills which he is not confident he can master, and he doesn't want to look silly. But building is clearly a man's job, and several lads he has known have worked on building sites, so he opts for building. And here we see him getting enormous satisfaction from exercising the manly skill of driving a dumper. True, he sometimes fancies his dumper is a racing car at Brands Hatch, but he is sufficiently in touch with reality to return to the dumper, and a demeanour appropriate to a dumper, when he thinks someone is looking. He is beginning to find that there are other kinds of satisfying manliness besides cheeking the teacher or truanting or even Paki-bashing. What his next step will be, who knows? One can imagine the kind of thing that might happen, and which in one form or another happens to many like him at the community. The builders have been asked to build (let us say) an incinerator. The instructor knows, almost in the twinkling of an eye, roughly how many bricks will be needed. How on earth does he do it? He is quite a tough, manly sort of person, and Tommy would like to be able to do the things he can do. He has by now discovered that the instructor is also friendly – even at times gentle – and approachable. So he simply asks him how he does it. The instructor is only too willing to oblige, but alas his task is made difficult by the fact that Tommy's knowledge of mensuration is so very limited. He doesn't even know how to find the area of a surface, much less work out cubic content. After struggling for a while the instructor has to admit that he hasn't time – with a dozen lads to supervise, working maybe at several different jobs – to explain the thing properly. 'But I'll tell you what. You know Gordon Godfree, don't you? He comes to your unit two or three evenings a week, and he's an expert at this sort of thing. Ask *him* one evening.' Certainly Tommy knows Gordon Godfree. Each member of the teaching staff has a secondary role, in the evenings or at weekends, in one of the living units. This gives them a chance to get to know the boys in a different context, and for the boys to get to know *them* simply as persons and not as pedagogues. So it is perfectly easy for Tommy to say one evening, 'Gordon! What the hell's a cubic foot?' Mr Godfree begins to explain, and he knows how to explain in a way that prevents a boy being too ashamed of his ignorance. But it's a bit tricky to get it all clear in the house in the evening, where Mr Godfree has perhaps other things to do, and a dozen or more boys are milling round, and without all the fascinating equipment he has in his workshop. So in due course – with no word having been said of 'school' or 'teacher' – Tommy is spending perhaps two mornings a week with Mr Godfree learning not only what the hell a cubic foot is, but experimenting also with all manner of absorbing things concerning number to which Mr Godfree can introduce him. And he will learn in weeks what his old school failed to teach him in as many years (see footnote on p. 99). The reason for this is simple. It is because the educators at the Community have the courage and the patience to wait until the boy is ready, and then to start from the point where *he* wants to begin.

The case of the mathematical dumper-driver is largely imaginary, but it is based on solid fact, and the staff of the Community know of many exactly like it. 'It's no use,' says Mike Jinks, 'sitting them in a classroom and then trying to push learning at them. They've totally rejected all that before they got here, so why try to fight that battle again? Start from where they're ready to begin, and go on from there. The concern that is shown for them in the living units will begin to give them a little security and hence a little confidence. Starting to work where they want to begin they will quickly acquire a sense of achievement and will further enhance their confidence. Then they will begin to move into other spheres.' 'But,' I said, 'you've only got them for eighteen months, and some of them are very infantile or very damaged. I can imagine such boys just beginning to move when it's time for them to go.' This apparently is often the case, but there are several answers to it. One is that the eighteen months is something the boy can extend if he so wishes, and some already do. But even if a boy cannot bring himself to ask for a further period at the Community, is it better to subject him to a regime which does nothing for him and then send him away untouched, or to provide him with something which just begins to open up possibilities that he can see? There was the case of Harry. He came to the Community quite illiterate. He was a grossly damaged boy and for eighteen months his resistance to schooling and his shame of his illiteracy prevented him coming anywhere near those who could have taught him to read. He did a bit of this, a bit of that, until one day he discovered an interest in clockwork machinery which one of the teachers shared. He 'played about' with clockwork until it was almost time for him to leave, and was then found a job with a watchmaker on which he entered while still living at the Community. It was now borne in upon him that whatever his skill as a watchmaker, he had no future in it so long as he was unable to read. Now there is on the staff of the Community a skilled teacher whose speciality is teaching those who are still at the infant level, whether this refers to academic attainment or emotional development. She lives in the town where Harry goes to work every day, and goes to the Community only three days a week. To her house Harry now goes during his dinner hour on the two days she is free, and at last he is learning to read. Like most of those who come late to primary learning his progress is rapid; but he realizes that he still has a good way to go before he is really fluent, so he has asked if he may remain at the Community a little longer.

I have said that there was nothing at the Community that Tommy recognized as school, and this was perhaps one of the greatest changes that was brought about by the new regime. Indeed the change of name from Cotswold School to Cotswold Community is evidence of the new attitude. Only very rarely is the cure for delinquency and emotional disorder to be found in what normally goes on in the classroom – and to do justice to the approved-school system, it has never assumed that this was the cure. Although most of them provided formal classroom work, they always talked of education *and training*, and by training they seem to have meant both the training of the character and training in a trade. But as we have seen, this concept had ceased to produce satisfactory results, and there are several things about the old approach that are now considered unhelpful. One we have looked at – it is no use trying to subject boys to formal education when they have already rejected it and will continue to resist it. The objections to the old 'trade-training' programmes are several, quite apart from the fact that in practice few boys followed in after-life the trade in which the school had begun to train them. (It must be remembered that I am speaking here of intermediate schools, dealing with roughly the thirteen to seventeen age group.) One criticism is that it seems to be assumed that if a boy is given a trade he will want to follow it in preference to his delinquent activities. This very *simple* attitude ignores the possibility that he might do both, and that he might carry on his trade in a delinquent way. There is also the great danger that if you establish trade departments – as most schools in the past have done – departments with workshops and work programmes in subjects like engineering, joinery, painting and decorating, gardening, farming, the work programme of the departments may gradually and insensibly become an end instead of a means, and the boys may become simply a means of keeping the workshops going.

One instructor in charge of such a department, who had been at Cotswold for many years, told me that in the old days the pressure of work that must be done was so great that his main problems were first to acquire a large enough number of boys, and then to keep them at it. In other words the thing had turned upside down and the boys served the departments instead of the departments serving the needs of the boys. It may be said of course that by putting a boy in circumstances that so nearly resemble industrial life you are preparing him for reality. But a large proportion of the boys who come to such a place as Cotswold have already rejected that kind of reality in the same way as they have rejected the reality of the classroom, and its acceptance is not brought about by forcing it upon them. In the old days it was thought that by keeping a boy hard at work you were training his character, but in fact if the character *can* be trained by rigorous discipline, it is successful only when it is voluntarily sought and entered into, and self-maintained. The Cotswold Community is not really concerned with training character. It is concerned with healing emotional wounds caused by affective deprivation, so that the character and personality can blossom and grow. Their purpose is, in an environment of overall care and concern for the individual, to provide the maximum number of opportunities for the development of the personality, and for the expression of that personality in a positive way.

Pursuing his purpose of delegating authority and pushing responsibility where it belongs, namely at the point of contact with the boy, Balbernie had appointed a man to organize the day-to-day activities of the boys. Trevor Blewett had already been appointed, as we have seen, to look after what one might call the home life of the boys, now Mike Jinks was appointed to concern himself with their working life. Remnants of the old terminology are perhaps to be seen in his title – head of education and training – but he brought to the work a totally new conception of the meaning of these words, and of the purpose of the programme; a conception reflected in the title by which he is now known – simply head of education. The purpose of the trade-training departments, he soon realized, should be exactly the same as the purpose of the classrooms, namely to provide opportunities for education in the broadest sense of the word. They must therefore all be brought within the ambit of a single organization, a single programme. No more compulsory hours in a classroom entirely separated from 'trade training'; no more division between 'teachers' and 'instructors' – all must be educators. No more classrooms, but just educational workshops with a skilled adult in attendance at each who has the equipment, both personal and material, to supply the needs of the boys who come to him. The kind of way in which they come to him we have already seen, and the new regime makes use in this educational way of all the kinds of employment that were available under the old regime, except two. One of these was farming. It was felt that the employment of

a large labour force on a farm was so completely out of touch
with the way that farm work is done in these days that for this
and other reasons the farm should revert to normal staffing and
procedures.*

The other was waiting on the staff. When the principal was
being shown over his house he was taken to the boiler room but
was told, 'No need to worry your head about that. One of the
boys looks after it.' The 'head's boiler-boy' had been employed
in stoking the head's boiler and doing other jobs about the
head's house, and in his spare moments carving his initials and
number on the inside of the boiler-room door. All this was
honest toil of which no one need be ashamed; what is hateful
about it is the assumption of a master–servant relationship between staff and inmates that is reminiscent of the old Poor Law;
and it highlights the danger of the purpose of the establishment
being lost in the need to keep the machinery going. A 'head's
boiler-boy' had to be appointed, and there must always be one,
not because it might be a useful educational or therapeutic
experience for a boy – though it might well be that in some
circumstances – but because the head's boiler had to be looked

---

* For twenty-five years these four hundred acres of Wiltshire land
were farmed with the primary purpose of training boys in farming.
It regularly employed forty or so boys, few of whom in fact took
up farming as a career, and as normally a farm of this size never
employs anything like that labour force, it was largely a matter of
'making' work for them, and it ran at a substantial loss. Making work
in this way is felt by the new regime to be neither realistic nor
educative and now that the farm is running on normal lines (and
beginning to show a profit!) there will be scope for the realistic
employment of a few boys who need and are ready for normal work
experience.

But it has also been invaluable as a *cordon sanitaire*, giving the
Community breathing space and elbow room and keeping them out
of their neighbours' hair, and they are eager to retain it for that
very important reason, if for no other.

Ivan Webster, the bailiff, has worked on the farm for twenty-five
years, and is as staunchly committed to the Community's primary
task as he is to his work as a farmer. The new regime sees many
possible social and educational uses for the farm – run as a successful farming enterprise – both for themselves and others, but up to
now these are perhaps no more than pipe dreams, so I will not dwell
on them.

after. So no more waiting upon the staff as part of the daily programme, though of course there is nothing to prevent a boy earning a couple of shillings in his spare time if he so chooses and someone wants his labour. If a boy comes to a staff member one evening and says, 'Clean your car for half-a-crown', that is an entirely different proposition from a boy being told at nine in the morning – 'Jones – go and clean Mr Smith's car.' Whether boys actually did clean staff members' cars as part of their daily work I do not know; but certainly there was a 'head's boiler-boy', which there no longer is, and equally certainly no boy dressed in blue check trousers and a white jacket now walks across the courtyard at eleven in the morning bearing a tray with a cup of coffee for the head. All that is gone.

The division between 'school' and 'training' was swept away, but one very clear division was made and insisted upon – the division between 'home' and 'work'. It was insisted that this division be made as clear, and the boundaries between them as distinct, as they are in ordinary life. Every boy, on leaving his unit to go to work in the morning (and they all talk about 'going to work', not going to school or, as in a hospital, 'going to OT'), feels himself to be crossing a real boundary into another world. A boundary so clear that it is possible for him to truant, which indeed some do. But a boy who does this knows that if he stays at home, or goes back home, his action will be sympathetically discussed with him by the home staff; there will be (in Jinks's words) 'An examination of his experience ... followed by a return to the education centre when he can handle the situation.' Or, as sometimes happens, 'home tuition' might be helpful for a week or two. We must remember that many of these fourteen year olds are at a stage of emotional development very much akin to that of a child of seven or eight or nine – not all, but many. A child of eight in a good home who finds something he cannot tolerate at school goes crying home to his mother, who will find a way of putting everything right again. This is exactly what happens here, except that the fourteen year old will probably not be crying, and when the matter is discussed he will be expected to make his contribution not only to the discussion of the problem but also to its solution. This is one of the reasons that the abscondance rate at the

Community is so much lower now than it once was.*

In 1969 they were talking about an 'educational centre'. It was difficult to find a name for this thing which was not school and was not trade training, but which incorporated the educational and therapeutic values of both; but the word was found, a word which describes it exactly, and which has no unpleasant associations for the boys. The word is 'Polytechnic'. I have explained how the 'living groups' were moved away from the central square and dispersed so far as possible on the periphery. A reverse process now took place. As the living groups moved away, the 'Poly' moved in. Instead of, as hitherto, workshops and classrooms dispersed about the place, they all moved into this quad at the heart of things, where even the man in charge of the garden has a room. By degrees the buildings on three sides of the square have been taken over (the fourth side is occupied by the back of buildings that front on to the other square). It is interesting, as well as instructive, to walk round them. To say that they are pretty tatty, at this point of time, is an understatement. But it must be remembered that they were fairly old and shabby to begin with, and that they were taken over for their new use the moment they were vacated. To wait until money and time were available to adapt them would have meant waiting for years for the completion of the plan, whereas now the Polytechnic is in being and the plan is in operation. The main building is I suppose the central one where Mike Jinks has his office. At right angles to this on one side is a building through the windows of which one can see coats of arms painted on the wall, and the symbols of various football clubs. This is the HQ of Fred Green and his painters and decorators,

---

*It is not to be assumed that boys who run away from approved schools or similar places are always seeking primarily to escape from a repressive environment, even when that environment *is* repressive. They are very often seeking to escape from inner conflict and anxiety, or signalling for help with those problems. One of the virtues of the present Cotswold organization is that a boy can do all that without actual abscondance with its attendant dangers. Boys will nevertheless continue to run away from time to time though at the time of writing there has not been a single case for seven months. Approved schools can usually expect that abscondances in a year will be something like a third or more of the population.

who spend part of their time there doing decorative painting and lettering (those of them who feel so disposed) and part of their time about the place doing necessary but non-urgent jobs of house-painting. This is done as and when the instructor thinks it will be useful to the boys. If it is something that must be done *now*, then it is done by maintenance staff or outside contractors. No one pretends that future painters and decorators are being trained, but – apart from any other considerations – the boys who have enjoyed this experience will certainly be able to make a better job of their own DIY house-painting when they have homes of their own. In a room above the painters is the silk-screen printing shop, which seems to be open as much in the evening as during the day. I was in one of the group homes one evening when a boy came rushing in in a great state of hurry and excitement.

'I want my T-shirt. Where's my T-shirt?'

'What are *you* doing then?'

'Silk-screen painting. You want to come, it's bloody good. *Come* on.'

'I'm just going off to the gym for some football.'

'Oh, bugger football. This is *good*, man. I'm going to print a design on my T-shirt' . . . and off he rushed.

Although it is considered of great importance to maintain a clear boundary between 'home' and 'work', this is a geographical and conceptual rather than a time boundary, and the aim is to have educational facilities available during evenings and weekends as well as during normal working hours. Many schools in the past have seen evening pursuits largely as a means of keeping boys out of mischief when they were not working, and every boy in such places has to be occupied at something or other. The Cotswold School had a very full evening programme including many admirable pursuits. But when under the new regime boys were told that they were perfectly free to attend or not as they pleased, attendance withered away – and boys complained, after the manner of adolescents everywhere, of having nothing to do. Cotswold now sees evening pursuits as part of the overall educational plan, in which a boy may partic-ipate in so far as, and only in so far as, his interest is aroused and maintained. In the old days the man in charge of an evening activity who did not see to it that interest was aroused, would suffer by having a group of bored and fractious boys on his hands. Now, such a man will have no boys at all! If a boy wants to spend the evening watching telly there is nothing to stop him. The surprising thing is how few boys *do* spend their evenings in this way, and the gratifying thing is to see the gradual erosion of that mortifying conception of work as a burden to be avoided if humanly possible.

But I have wandered from the Polytechnic. Along the passage from silk-screen printing is a room containing sacks of potatoes, some gardening tools, and on the walls some charts about plant development and botany. This is the headquarters of rural science, though obviously most of the work is done elsewhere, and here again it is planned for education and not for production, though production may well take place, both for the Community and for individual boys who may want their own garden plot. Coming downstairs again at the other end one finds a couple of canoes made at the Community and used on one of the gravel-pit 'lakes', among other places.

Across the square from this wing is a similar wing which was the latest to be taken over. The boys had ceased living in it and moved to other quarters only a couple of weeks before I saw it, but the Poly had moved in, and while much of it was still bare and empty at that time, one large room was occupied by an elaborate model railway, the track of which weaved in and out, up and down, all over the place. This looked more like play than work; but I am reminded that the Community is often dealing with boys who – however big – are still at the small-boy stage of development, and very often the play way is the only way to get them started. Once again I am impressed by the courageous confidence and patience of the Polytechnic staff, who are prepared to let a boy 'play at trains' until he is ready for the next step.

The central building between these two wings is the important one. Not because the head of education has his office there, but because it was the first to be taken over, and is more full of fascinating activities than either of the others. Here is to be found, on the ground floor, David Gilbert, the sculptor, and for the boys who come to him sculpture is not a grim matter of chipping away with a hammer and cold chisel, though that may be part of it. He can introduce them to ways of putting their imagination to work in a score of mediums, from an old lump of timber out of the rubbish tip to the entrails of a piano – from the same source. And the end-products vary from romantic female figures to complicated looking things in the latest style of twisted wire and nails; or, indeed, to some very sophisticated furniture making. There are power tools here, and often there is a boy or two from another group who wants to drill a couple of holes or use the sander on the bedside bookcase he is making. In another room is Tony Wakeham the potter, with a treadle wheel but as yet no kiln, but that has not prevented the making of an enormous variety of 'thrown' or modelled objects. You will not see these objects, nor the sculpture nor anything else that has been finished. When a boy has made something it is his, and he takes it away to show with pride first to the people in his living unit, and later to his family. So you will not see a collection of those museum pieces that one sometimes sees on display in such places, gathering the dust of ages and making one wonder why the people who made them didn't take them home, and whether anything like them has ever been made since.

Still on the ground floor in a couple of rooms at the back is Ian Shaw with the engineers. Their tools and equipment are minimal; there is no forge, though Mr Shaw lives in hope. But he is the sort of man who can work wonders with a couple of spanners and a hacksaw and, while he has a few more tools than that, he knows that if he had insisted that elaborate equipment was essential it would not have been possible to start the shop for another year or more. But he sees more educational value in improvisation and make-it-yourself than in an expensively equipped workshop. Here boys can do any kind of metal work (entirely with scrap metal), but the main interest seems to be automobile engineering. I saw four old motor cycles on which boys were working with great seriousness and enthusiasm – all rescued from the scrapheap. Here go-karts and all manner of other weird vehicles have been made, including a raft for the lake. If you want to know what c.c. means, or if you need a drawing of what you are going to make, then Gordon Godfree or Barry Rogers upstairs can help you. The walls of their rooms are covered with interesting charts and diagrams and geological and botanical specimens. They have paper, pencils, books and rulers and all the ordinary requirements of orthodox schooling, but they have also various gadgets to help you to understand – many of them home-made, like the teaching machines which enable a boy to have the experience of teaching himself and correcting his own work as he goes along. Their rooms are as unlike the kind of classrooms the boys are familiar with as can be imagined – they are just as much workshops as the engineering shop or the sculpture room. All teaching of the basic subjects (and much else besides that goes on here) is informal and individual, and is provided as and when it is asked for. In still another room upstairs is the printing shop where you can make your own Christmas cards, or help to do jobs of printing for the Community.

Along the passage again is Mrs Whitmore. She runs, you might almost say, the nursery school. She is there for three days each week, and is an outstanding example of the way in which the Cotswold insists on providing what the children need, however bizarre those needs might seem to the uninformed. She is by training and experience an infant teacher. While perhaps very few of the boys are still at the infant level of attainment, several of them are at a very early stage of emotional development. In nursery school and infant classes perhaps more than anywhere else one sees children being accepted for exactly what they are, each with his own unique experiences, and that unique experience being used as a starting-point for further experience. This is in general the Cotswold kind of education, so it seems likely that an infant teacher would not only understand it, but would be able to apply it with skill to those who were still emotionally infants. Fortunately this particular infant teacher, who has reared a large family, also understands adolescents (I suspect she is not unique among infant teachers in this; there is much in common between those just entering life and those just entering maturity), so she is able to supply infantile needs without offending adolescent susceptibilities. She is accustomed to exercising an authority which is not dependent upon a system or an organization, but comes directly from

herself, expressing itself with warmth and affection, and gener-
ating a feeling of safety and security rather than provoking
rebelliousness. She operates through media as diverse as soft-toy
making and cookery, but among it all manages also to encourage
those who are at the earliest stages of letter and number.

All these activities – and probably several I have not men-
tioned – are going on in the Polytechnic, but this is by no means
the whole of the educational work. We have seen how each of
the Polytechnic staff spend an evening or two a week in one
of the living groups – not, be it said, as teacher, but as relief for
child-care staff off duty. But while he is there, whatever his reason for being there, and whatever his function in that context,
there is nothing to prevent him from communicating his en-
thusiasms, from talking to boys about the things he is interested
in, of giving them help, as an educator, with the things that
interest them. I found a teacher in one unit in the evening with
a set of bamboo musical pipes he was helping boys to make.
We have seen also how in some cases boys can pursue those
interests at the Poly in the evenings. One gets the impression
that the engineers shop, for example, is never closed, so that a
boy who has got a motor-bike to the point where it is almost
ready for the road can rush back after tea and finish the job.
Ian Shaw says that although as often as not there is no adult
there in the evening, he has not yet lost a tool. But even this is
not all. Many of the boys who come to the Community may
have distinguished themselves in the subculture of the delinquent world and the street corner, by their delinquent acts,
their daring and their aggressiveness; but in relation to
society as a whole they are failures, and they can be highly
sensitive about their failure. I have referred to the boy who
could not bring himself to seek help over his reading until he
was almost due to leave. The work of the Community is successful, broadly speaking, only in so far as a boy is able to establish
a good, intimate, affective relationship with at least one adult.
Very often that adult is the only one he feels able to approach
about his problems, and if the problem is an educational one,
it may well be that at first that person is the only one from
whom he can accept teaching. Even those of us who have good
loving homes, and are relatively stable and well integrated, find

it easier to accept teaching from someone we like or admire. Very many of the kind of boy who comes to the Cotswold find it quite impossible to accept teaching from anyone else. So all the staff – whatever their primary function – have to be prepared to receive these shy appeals for help, and everyone, within the limits of his skill and knowledge, has to be prepared to do some personal individual teaching. Not, in most cases, for very long. It is the start that is important. Once this has been made, the boy will soon be ready to move on to another person with the specific skills and equipment that the boy needs – and the time to use them.

The Polytechnic buildings, while pleasant enough externally, are inside shabby almost to the point of decrepitude – I have explained that they were taken over for their present use immediately they ceased to be used for other purposes, with only the minimum, absolutely essential adaptation. But I do not think anyone can walk through those shabby rooms without experiencing the feeling – as I always do – that here is something real, something vital. Here boys who had in despair sought distinction in the subculture of violence and delinquency were discovering the possibility of being real men; men acceptable not only to one small cut-off group, but to the world at large; here unhappy children were learning to grow up into happy, purposeful adults.

This impressive atmosphere of growth and vitality was created by the men – and woman! – who worked there; people of outstanding calibre who have gradually been recruited, or who have been retained from the previous dispensation. To say that they are enthusiastic about what they are doing is perhaps to give the wrong impression. Enthusiastic they certainly are, but in a quiet, unaggressive, unassuming kind of way, which plods on deterred neither by the fractious and intractable nature of the young people with whom they are concerned, nor by the many material setbacks and obstacles which have confronted and still confront them.

The dilapidated state of the building was not due only to the speed with which the conversion was effected; it was due also to the shortage of money referred to earlier, and the quality of the staff is revealed in the manner in which those at the

Polytechnic faced this challenge. A sculptor – David Gilbert – joined the staff, but as there was no money available just then he set up a workshop with his own tools, some wood of his own, and such scraps of sculptable or constructable material as he could pick up about the estate – mostly from the rubbish dump. Several exciting objects were constructed with material from this source and nine months passed before any money was available for this activity. Ian Shaw, the engineer, was unwilling – even if the money had been there – to indent for costly things like lathes until he could see how the thing was going to develop, and the work I described (page 110) was all created with a derisory few pounds' worth of tools, and a great deal of scrap metal. Tony Wakeham the potter, like others of the staff, was recruited because he had much to offer and was available; the question of financing his work had to be gone into after he got there, and the fact that at first there wasn't any money did not seem to worry him at all. I have said that he had a treadle wheel but no kiln. This is not strictly accurate. There had been a kiln for some time, but frost disintegrates it every winter and it has to be rebuilt every summer. The wheel was entirely home-made, except for the actual spinning disc. The flywheel was made by pouring concrete in an old tyre, the treadle was the back of an old chair, the wooden framework was constructed from bits of timber picked up about the estate. He gets his clay by digging it by hand. The pottery shop cost twenty pounds in its first year. When an enterprising young artist wanted to do silk-screen printing Jinks had to say, 'Sorry, no money.' The young man went back to his art college (where he was still working part-time) and so infected students and staff with his own enthusiasm that they between them made possible the episode described on page 108.

The men I have referred to as having been 'recruited' came to the Cotswold because they felt themselves to be in accord with its general approach and were glad to find an opportunity to pursue their own interests in a sympathetic environment. They were recruited in the usual way through advertisements in the appropriate journals, but as time passed an increasing number made their own approaches because they had heard what was going on and wanted to share in it. Others were recruited from among men and women on Home Office child-care courses who, having spent a short period at the Community on practical work placements, now wanted to return there to work. Presumably, in spite of the difficulties (perhaps even because of them), they are happily fulfilling themselves. But what of those to whom I referred as having been 'retained' – the several who joined the staff years ago under the old dispensation? They came to work in a very different setting, and they have shown their calibre in the way they have been able to adapt to the new ways. The process of change and adjustment was an immensely trying one, one that would in any case have subjected them to considerable emotional stress; but while they were suffering the throes of adaptation they were also called upon to endure the contempt and hostility of some of their colleagues, who were unwilling or unable to attempt that adaptation. Simultaneously to make that adjustment and to suffer that animosity betokens great stature and great integrity. The same disaffection and enmity was directed at the head of education as his intentions were revealed; this was a repetition of what had been suffered by others and which I have already discussed. Something like twelve months had passed before Jinks could feel that he had anything like a united staff.

Whether that staff was 'recruited' or 'retained', their task is onerous and stressful. It makes enormous demands on a man, and if he has become accustomed to leaning on the structure of formal discipline he finds the experience of relying on his own resources frightening and exhausting – and this is true not only of those who had been at the Cotswold in the old days; it is equally true of those who have come there recently. It is always true that the absence of a formal structure, the patient waiting for the right moment, waiting for needs to be felt, and then attempting to supply those needs in a rather intimate, often one-to-one setting, seeking always to find a way of presenting it that is acceptable to the pupil – then often finding it rejected and having to start again from another angle; all this is demanding in the extreme, and a man must have a good measure of personal stability to be able to cope with it. It is immeasurably easier just to stand in front of a disciplined class and 'throw it at them', and even the best of us can, in these new circumstances, find our security threatened and our resources stretched.

One of the important things that is only now being learned in the fields of child care and education is that it is not enough merely to examine the effect that the worker and his efforts have upon the child; it is of no less importance to examine and understand what the children – and the methods used – are doing to the adults. To help the Polytechnic staff in all this an educational consultant meets with them once a fortnight. This is Mr Ronald Dare, Senior Educational Psychologist to the Wiltshire County Council, and a very old friend of Richard Balbernie's. With Mr Dare they discuss their problems, not only at the level of knowing (which we used to think education was all about), but also at the level of feeling. They find that this is no less difficult than doing the job itself, but there is no doubt that its value to them will be enormous. Particular examination, says Jinks, is made by the child of the staff's ability to make relationships, and to use their subject-matter as a way of promoting those relationships, rather than as a defence in an organizational system. Again, the capacity to 'read' behaviour and to respond not merely to that but also to the need of which it may be an expression – this is a skill that comes only with time, with painful experience and with much self-knowledge. In all this they are helped by the educational consultant.

One more thing needs to be said about the Polytechnic and the efforts that are made to prepare boys to return to ordinary life. We saw a few pages back how Harry was going to work every day in the neighbouring town, and he is not the only one. It has been strongly felt all along that it was unwise to plunge the boys straight from the security of Community life into the double hazard of returning home and starting work. All good schools catering for 'normal' children living at home do what they can to prepare them for industrial life, and this is done partly in the classroom and partly through visits or observation.

However successful this may be with normal children, it is inadequate for those living in institutions of any kind, or for those who are emotionally disturbed or inadequate. This I have seen repeatedly in my own experience with boys leaving schools for maladjusted children. They often left school full of intelligent and praiseworthy ideas of how they intended to conduct themselves in relation to earning a living, but because these were ideas that had been presented to them rather than acquired as a result of their own experience, they did not long survive the reality of working life.*

The Cotswold tries to avoid this breakdown (which can have tragic consequences) by providing normal work experience while the boy is still living in the secure conditions of the Community, still among trusted people who can help him to interpret and evaluate his experience. At the time I am writing not many boys have enjoyed this experience because the time-scale has militated against it. Little would be gained by pushing a boy out to battle with employment – even from the security of the Community – while he is still so disturbed that he is unable to cope with it, and it has frequently happened hitherto that by the time a boy has been ready for this experience, it has been time for him to leave. With the ending of the approved-school order, bringing a much more flexible time-scale, this will tend to sort itself out, though there will remain a similar and cognate problem. Ideally the Community needs to have a boy twelve to eighteen months before school-leaving age, so that there is some hope that he may have acquired a measure of stability and ego strength by the time he is due to start work. Unfortunately, however, delinquent behaviour occurs much more frequently during the last year at school than in the year or two preceding it, and there is thus constant pressure on intermediate schools to take boys who are near the top of the age range for which they cater. It is possible that this situation too may be relieved in the future by two factors; with the end of the approved-school system as we know it there is no reason to assume that the present division into junior, intermediate and senior schools will necessarily continue on its present basis; and with the raising of the school-leaving age to sixteen, there is good reason to suppose that that particular 'delinquency peak' will go up with it, as it appears to be associated rather with the fact of school-leaving than with age itself.

It was when the idea of the Polytechnic had been conceived and was in all the throes of struggling to establish itself that

*See W. David Wills, *A Place Like Home*, Allen & Unwin, 1970.

some members of the Community staff happened to visit an exhibition at the Cirencester Library. It had been arranged by a consortium of local authorities who were proposing to establish an extensive 'water park' in and around the 'lakes' formed by the many large worked-out gravel beds which stretch for miles in this part of the country. It is a splendid and imaginative project and the Community staff, as local residents, were naturally interested in it. By the time they had examined the large and beautiful maps on the wall of the library their interest was enhanced, but it was coupled with dismay and consternation. Right across the Cotswold Community's premises, in letters of red, were the words 'Site of proposed caravan park', and in the beautiful, illustrated brochure is a note which reads, 'There is a possibility that land to the east of this pit, the Cotswold Community, may be acquired by the Wiltshire County Council and be included in Keynes Park. This location would be suitable for the establishment of a transit or holiday caravan park.' 'So *that*,' they said to each other, 'is why Wiltshire is interested in the Community. They hope to acquire it not in order to further the experiment to which we are committed, but simply for the benefit of their water park. *Then* what happens to the Community – and what happens to us?'

They may have been wrong in this assumption, however obvious it seemed, and officials of the County Council assured Balbernie with great sincerity that they were, and it was all a misunderstanding. But it is much easier to raise fears of that kind than it is to allay them, and this was a further addition to the load of worry and anxiety which Balbernie was carrying quite independently of the worries and anxieties inherent in the primary job he had come to the Cotswold to do. Worries and anxieties furthermore that were not now peculiar to him, but affected all those who had come there to work with him. He knew of one man only who might be strong enough and influential enough to prevent this catastrophe if it were indeed what it seemed, namely Derek Morrell, and to him he now prepared to turn for help and advice. It was at this point – though still only in his forties – that Morrell died; an irreparable loss not only to Balbernie and the Cotswold Community, but to all deprived and 'delinquent' children everywhere.

# 7 A Man's World?

The reader who is well informed in the field of activities with which this book is concerned may well have been asking why so little has been said about the role of women in the Cotswold Community. One reason for this is that I propose to devote a whole chapter to the subject; another is that their role is by no means yet established. Indeed, the fact that women can be written about in this separate way is a symptom of their rather primitive status up to now. One might almost write about 'the woman problem' as Edwardian journalists did when the movement for the emancipation of women was just beginning. Women at the Cotswold are not yet wholly emancipated, and when I say this I say it in all possible charity, I say it not in criticism of the women, but – if of anyone – of the men. It is still very much a man's world at the Cotswold, though very much less so than it once was, and much is being done to remedy this situation which everyone, including those who unconsciously contribute to it, deplores. In my own view it is perhaps in this sphere that the least progress has been made, though this is not for want of trying. When I have visited the various living units at the Community I have several times had a most revealing experience. On entering one is very warmly received by whatever man happens to be on duty, one is shown round, introduced to such boys as are about the place, and to other men. After a while one will see the dim figure of a young woman flitting across the background, perhaps crossing a passage from one room to another, and a conversation something like this will ensue.

'Who's the pretty girl?'

'Oh – er – yes, haven't you met her? That's Jane' (or Sally or Jean or whatever it might be) 'our housemother. Very nice girl. First class. Absolutely great . . .'

I pursue the topic of housemothers further, if I feel strong enough and my interlocutor is sufficiently encouraging, and eventually he will say, 'Would you like to meet her?'

All this speaks volumes, and I need not comment on it. I find it rather sad, but it is an enormous improvement on the early days. The Cotswold School with its 120 boys, had an establishment of four housemothers, though only one was in her post at the time of the changeover, and there was no woman teacher. The aim at present is to have, when opportunity presents itself, at least one more woman teacher (there is one at present) and two housemothers in each living unit. Pat Drew, whose official style and title is resident social-case worker, is in practice the person responsible for developing the women's side of the work and for supervising those parts of the Community's activities that are carried out by women. This is thought of as a more or less temporary role for Pat, because when women are properly integrated into the life of the place – as clearly they will be eventually – this separate concern for their welfare and separate regard of their duties will no longer be appropriate or necessary. But up to now it has been.

Pat Drew tells a story of the early days which, as indicating the point from which they began, shows also how far they have progressed. Pat was at this time the only, or almost the only, trained woman on the staff (she has teaching and child-care training and experience) though there were, as there always had been, daily cleaners and sempstresses. The boys were still living in the large houses whose façades looked on to the square, and Pat heard that there was a sick boy in one of the houses. She went over to investigate. Yes, she was told, it was true that there was a boy in bed.

'Right,' said Pat, 'I'll go and have a look at him and take his temperature.'

The man to whom she was speaking was horrified.

'*What*,' he said, 'you can't do *that*.'

'Why not?'

'Well of course you can't. A *woman* can't go into the boys' dormitories!'

'Then it's about time they did, and I'm going into this one.'

The altercation continued for a little while, but eventually Pat ascended to the forbidden area, preceded by one man to prepare the way, and followed by another, presumably as rearguard. Such an incident, as we shall see, could not possibly happen now, so there is progress. Bedtime is a time of vital importance to children in residential care, a time which tends to reactivate all their anxieties and fears about separation and desertion. At bedtime, therefore, housemothers will be seen, with their male colleagues, giving such reassurance as they can, tucking up, taking round hot bedtime drinks, perhaps just talking. Undoubtedly there is progress, but not as much as they hope to see.

In discussing the role of the woman, it is helpful to remind ourselves of the man's. This is to provide a good model for the adolescents who are approaching manhood, and, by his personal authority, to 'hold' the disturbed and erratic young people while they are learning how to cope themselves with their own wayward impulses; while they are learning how to make positive, constructive use of their own male aggression; learning to feel concern for others The woman's role is equally vital, equally necessary, and provides for needs equally pressing. She too helps to provide security by enhancing the feeling of being cared for in the feminine, mothering kind of way. The adolescent boy – even the normal adolescent boy – is in a sense living through a second infancy because he is entering life, the adult life, just as he was entering life then, and at this stage is liable to make many emotional demands upon his mother or upon any appropriate mother-figure that happens to be at hand. Disturbed adolescents have frequently suffered grave impairment of the mother–child relationship, and the role of the woman worker is to be the target of feelings displaced from the mother to her, to understand them, and by skilled and patient understanding to help the boy to work through them. Some boys have been denied much or all of that primary mother–child experience without which we cannot go forward to become separate, 'other-regarding' individuals. In such cases the woman worker has to try to provide those primary experiences. All this is not only highly skilled work, it is work which puts them at the receiving end of much displaced animosity and hatred, which they have to accept and help the child, again, to work through if he is to make progress. In many such cases it is this primitive dependent relationship with a woman which enables a boy later to accept what is being offered by other people or other experiences.

They too must provide a model, a model however not of one kind of person but of two; a model not of what he is to become, but of the qualities he is to look for in girl-friend and wife, and in a mother for his children.

When they properly understand and appreciate each other's role and function, men and women colleagues in a residential unit are of great help to each other in 'getting into role', and in a sense justify each other. The man who is really masculine and provides real authority ensures by that means a 'safe' area in which the woman can work. If he does not provide that authority she on the one hand feels insecure and somewhat thwarted, and at the same time feels called upon to supply what he has failed to supply, becoming perhaps nagging or domineering and thus unable to be her real feminine self. If the man gives too much expression in his work to the feminine side they will tend to see each other as rivals and role confusion may arise, causing uncertainty and a reduced sense of security among the boys. Not for one moment is it suggested that the feminine side – which every man has, as every woman has a masculine – should never find expression; much less is it suggested that tenderness and concern are more feminine than masculine. They are human attributes, and are not peculiar to either sex. If sex differentiation enters into it at all it is shown in the mode of expression, and perhaps in the degree of importance, or at least priority, attached to it. There is a proper balance and proportion in these things, and it is likely that on the whole boys find it easier to demand and to receive this sort of thing from women, though this is by no means a universal rule. It is essential that they understand and recognize each other's particular gifts and capacities and encourage each other in their expression without envy or jealousy and without either attempting to dominate the scene. This mutual sympathy, support and respect are absolutely imperative if the boys are not to be given a repetition of the inter-sexual discord and contempt for the female which has so often been a feature of their early life. It is not necessary openly to quarrel in order to create this repetition. The probability is that many of the boys will be expecting to find it, and it will only need a hint, a slightly derogatory word, a momentary failure of respect, for them to assume that here, as at home, war is the natural state between the sexes.

The masculine role as now understood at the Cotswold was, as we saw, little understood by most of the men who were there at the changeover, and by no means fully understood by the new men who came; and we saw something too of the battle (it was no less) to get this conception understood and accepted. It was not easy to put across, and once accepted by the men it was not easy for them to learn how to exercise it. It is not surprising therefore if in the stress and worry of understanding and trying to practise their own function, they did not have time or inclination to acquire a proper understanding of someone else's, namely that of their women colleagues, and many of them, while making progress in their own role, tended to remain stuck with the old-fashioned primitive idea of the woman as simply a domestic provider. All this is changing but the change is one that involves the undermining of very old and deep-rooted concepts and prejudices, and this cannot be done as quickly as one might wish. That the woman should be in part a domestic provider is right and good – it is part of her role. One might say that whereas other professional women are, so far as their work is concerned, asexual – they are doctors or lawyers or teachers first and women second – the woman in residential child care is not so much a *professional* woman as a professional *woman*, and the recognition and acceptance of her in the primary woman role by the boys is helped when they see her doing those things they associate with women; that she should be nothing else is quite preposterous because it is so limiting as to be crippling.

Pat Drew and her pioneer women (for that is how I think of them in this man's world) were therefore faced with the frightening problem of infiltrating a male stronghold, where at first they were frankly not wanted, in order to carry out with inadequate numbers a task that was of great difficulty and complexity and intensely demanding, among reluctant colleagues who had little idea what they were up to. It was not that the men were actually hostile to their women colleagues, but that hitherto the role of women in the school had been simply that of domestic providers, and it had never been suggested to them that there was a place for women as professional therapeutic colleagues. To those who were opposed in any case to the changed conception of the establishment's function it was just another new-fangled notion to resent.

In carrying out this thankless and arduous task the first problem was to find the personnel. It was too much to hope that the requisite number of suitably trained women could be found immediately, but in the meantime there were women already on the staff, and any woman, whether or not she understands exactly what is being done at the Cotswold, can see the need for things like flowers on the table and all those other touches that women provide and which make the difference between living and civilized living. These women were for the most part 'dailies' – cleaners, laundresses, sempstresses, cooks, and the devoted, gentle and competent Miss Crump, who had served the Cotswold with loyalty and fidelity in a matroning capacity for nearly a quarter of a century. These, with two new housemothers who had been found, were taken into the confidence of the new management and told something of what it was hoped to do, and how the contribution they were already making could be even greater. Together they looked at the Community to see how they could best inject a little feminine softness and a little feminine grace into this rough, hard world of men. It had never occurred to some of them that this could be any of their business, and when their opinion and their help were sought they became different people. 'I don't like to say this really,' said one of them, 'but we all feel it. I wish we could find a way of doing more.' No longer shadowy background figures who came merely to provide so many hours of cleaning or sewing, they revealed their true selves, ordinary human persons with something to give. Some of them were moved over experimentally to a partial housemother role to see whether they could accept – and carry out – the idea of providing for boys' emotional needs instead of just domestic services, and there were those among them who for a time made a real contribution in this sphere. There was a good deal of trial and error, and looking back on those days Pat Drew says the main problem seemed often to be that of removing women who were unable to cope with the tensions and stresses of their new and enlarged role. But they made a beginning, they held the fort in some sort of way while trained, professional women were being found.

The real breakthrough came from a quite unexpected quarter and it was a breakthrough not only in the matter of women's role, but in the general 'softening' of the whole place. In the search for feminine help some young Community Service Volunteer girls had been introduced, partly because of the general difficulty of finding suitable women, but also because it was thought that some young attractive girls about the place would help to normalize this masculine environment. They were a resounding success. They were a success indeed partly because of their lack of training and experience. They had no preconceived ideas, no traditions, no axes to grind. They were just perfectly natural girls, and they were encouraged to be just that, though not without some warning about the difficulties they might expect to meet, and not without a good deal of encouragement when those difficulties arose. They each stayed six months or a year, and from that time the Community has never been without its quota of CSV girls. Sometimes they bring problems with them and sometimes they create problems; this is only to be expected when young, inexperienced and mainly middle-class girls are put down among a mass of rough, inconsiderate, delinquent boys. But it did the trick; it was their presence that made the move towards a gentler and more civilized mode of living possible.

Outstanding among them in the early days was a blind girl of eighteen who with great courage and integrity, making no use whatever of her affliction to gain pity, sympathy or special treatment, received from these deprived and brutal boys not only displaced animosity, crudely expressed, but even ill-natured abuse about her blindness. Yet her persistent gentleness found its way to a corresponding quality – deeply buried, rarely expressed, self-despised – in these rough and apparently unfeeling boys. She was sitting beside one of them in the small sitting room of the Cottage one evening. He was rolling a cigarette, and when she became aware of this she said something to the effect that she supposed this was a thing she couldn't do. He replied, as he usually did, with stupid but wounding abuse for a while, then paused, and said in a rough, embarrassed way, 'You can.' She, surprised, asked him what he meant – how did he know what she could and couldn't do? He replied – and what a world of significance was in his reply – 'I practised it in bed for two hours last night with my eyes shut.' Behind all his truculent ill-nature he had been aware of her, had put himself in her place, had, in however limited a manner, sympathized with her, had tried to find out what it was like to be blind.

I do not say that a man could not evoke such a response. I was in the Cottage twelve months later when the softening-up process was much further advanced and another blind CSV worker was introduced. This one was a young man, and it was touching to see the concern and solicitude of some at least of the boys. But it is something that comes much more readily and naturally in a woman, and is a vital part of her role in a place like the Cotswold Community.

CSV girls, whatever their virtues, are not an adequate substitute for permanent, trained women who can do all that not merely 'by the light of nature' but with conscious professional insight; the search for such women continued – and continues. Throughout the whole period the problem has been first to find and then to keep girls who are doing this demanding and exhausting work in a physical environment that is very remote and, in winter, rather desolate. It was soon realized that one woman in each unit was not enough, and the establishment now aimed at is two professional child-care women to each group. At this moment there is at least one such person in each unit, usually a young, attractive girl who can do much to normalize the atmosphere and is an essential part of any such community in order to maintain a rational balance of age and sex – but she can hardly take a maternal place with teenage boys. These girls are a first-class team and are acquiring, in addition to their previous training, an understanding of their function at the Cotswold Community. Although they are not old enough to be mother-figures, this does not inhibit the boys from displacing upon them a good deal of ill-feeling and hatred, in addition to the more acceptable attitudes that an adolescent boy can be expected to show to an attractive girl. All this is new to them, they are young and they are lonely. Though the days when their mere presence was resented are happily past, and although the men understand much better than they once did how valuable is the contribution they can make, one feels that their acceptance is still rather a surface acceptance in many cases, that they are not yet fully integrated into the unit team. It is essential that there should be, in addition to these young girls, an older woman in each unit, one who can support her younger colleague and can take more naturally a mother role. This, at the time I write, the Community is striving desperately to achieve and there is no doubt that when they are found the final integration of women into the unit team will be easier to bring about.

By way of illustrating the role and function of women in a therapeutic community I give below some extracts from the detailed narrative records that were kept about two boys, by the women to whom they were particularly attached. These two workers were women, doing women's work, but in doing it they express a great deal of what is essential and intrinsic in the work of the Cotswold, by whomsoever carried out – the skilful use of relationships, the unfailing and unconditional affection, coupled with complete non-colluding rejection of anti-social behaviour.

The first notes concern Charlie, a relatively integrated but very neurotic boy of fourteen. The notes were made by a young married woman with no previous experience and no training except such as she had picked up at the Community. That training was largely through the medium of on-the-job discussions with the social-case worker of specific problems as they arose, and of course the weekly meetings with the therapeutic consultant. I have extracted not quite at random, but almost so.

*Sixth month after arrival.* Charlie has lately become very homesick. From certain things that he says about home, although he feels completely rejected now, I feel he earlier received a lot of love and attention, and this he misses very much (this love seems to have been transferred to his younger brother). He tries to be very hard at times but I am sure this is to cover up his inner softness. He likes a great deal of feminine attention although he tries not to show it, particularly in the presence of male staff. Says he misses home and now very often talks of running off. As he watches me doing things like sewing, etc., he always relates it to his mother's actions. I should imagine he has spent quite a lot of time with his mother, helping her with sewing, knitting, etc. In the presence of other boys he will sometimes speak ill of his mother, but perhaps this is an effort to shake off the strong attachment he has to her.

*Seventh month.* Although Charlie is very clever with his hands and can tackle a man's job, it seems to me he is missing more and more his mother's love. He spends quite a lot of time with me, sometimes just sitting quietly, and if I am sewing he will sometimes pick up a needle and cotton and start sewing, or help himself to some wool and make pompoms. He shows a certain amount of jealousy when boys make things for me, goes out of his way to make something better.

He spent one evening sleeping downstairs on the settee, after first of all lying under a cupboard for some time, and although it appears to be girl-friend trouble, I think he was really after individual attention for when I went to him later, he made it very clear that he was still there.

He also went off briefly and returned this month, and when he came back said he hadn't known where he was going – he just kept on walking. He covers up a great deal of his feelings by being noisy and saying things are 'a great laugh'.

Recently I have taken him, with others, to a youth club and in company, particularly female, he is very shy. He either covers his face under his jumper or projects a mouthful of seemingly un-thoughtful words. At bedtime he is a completely different person, showing softness and childlikeness. He shares a room with two boys who are attention-seeking and Charlie is very hurt if he doesn't receive the same attention, but if one of his 'tough' friends appears on the scene, he immediately becomes hard again.

*Eighth month.* He admits that he cannot yet be responsible for him-self and says he preferred the staff to tell him what to do, because he thinks this is the only way he will be taught not to get his own way. Also said 'A good hiding might do me good.'

The fact that Charlie can barely read or write is becoming a big problem to him. In front of others he will say he is not interested in learning but in one of his sensible moments he said he would really like to learn more, but would never go in the schoolroom because he was afraid of showing himself up. However, he said he would like to spend half an hour each day reading aloud to himself if he could be sure no one was listening. He is completely resistant to any formal situation and needs sensitive, informal help, not thrust at him but available when he feels able to make use of it. If it was organized for him he would resist it completely.

[Note by social-case worker – *Indirect* educational help and availability so far through the worker making these notes, has been essential. Gradually, however, in gaining confidence, first in carpentry and more recently in engineering, mainly motor-cycle repairs, it has been possible to enfold this in developing vocational interest.]

*Ninth month.* On his own volition he has started to copy out the words of pop songs into a book, and although he insists that he can't read or write, his writing in this book is quite good, and although he is reluctant to admit it I think he is quite proud of his effort.

*Tenth month.* Education is another thing which makes him feel very inferior in comparison with his brother. After his accident with the chisel he wrote a letter to his mother. He let me look at it and said that it was so bad that he supposed I couldn't read a word of it. I gathered he was pleased when I read it without hesitation, but he continued to say Gary's writing was very neat, that he could write twice as fast, and that one would never find a spelling mistake in his letters.

Charlie's feelings are hidden from most people. When confronted with a question he invariably replies with the 'don't care' or 'I don't know' type of answer, without first of all stopping to think what his real answer is, and if he is misunderstood becomes hurt and aggressive. He is not very often at ease with his friends either, but tries to act and talk in the way in which he thinks he is expected to. However, since he has shared a room with a smaller boy he is completely at ease in his presence and enjoys normal conversation, and is not afraid to show the soft side of his personality.

The feeling of inferiority seems to be Charlie's biggest problem, which seems to be emphasized when he is told to do something. He always resents being told to do anything and it seems to me that by taking this attitude to him it is the same as telling him he is incapable of thinking for himself. For example, if I tell him he needs a haircut he will disagree violently, but if I ask him to let me know when he wants a haircut he invariably makes a decision within a couple of days. He is very useful doing practical things and to ask his opinion on these lines gives him more confidence and helps him to chat naturally, instead of blurting out a mouthful of words which really mean nothing.

*Twelfth month.* Some of his communication with me is in a type of code; e.g. if something is bothering him he will not ask if he could speak to me, but will either lock himself in the housemother's room, refuse to go to bed, or ask me to wash his hair so as to speak in private; if he wants a second kiss at bedtime he will keep saying, 'Good-night' till he gets one, and if he wants to say he is sorry after an argument he will make contact by asking simple questions to which he already knows the answer.

My second extracts, concerning William, are from notes made by another worker, and are about a very institutionalized, emotionally deprived and unintegrated little boy of fifteen, who had been cruelly ill-treated as a victim of the subculture tyranny. In this case I have simply copied almost verbatim the first third of the notes.

Very little initial contact this week, apart from asking for a jar for his frogspawn, which he came to show me with great delight. He came to my flat to see TV and sat very rigidly watching 'Top of the Pops'. At bedtime William enjoys stories, he asked for 'Jack and Jill, I like that.' He asked me to go to Scottish Dancing and made a great display of 'heavy' dancing.

A very ambivalent week of feelings, sometimes a demure child – seeking relationships gently and quietly – at other times violent, rude, almost sadistic. William has a collection of pins, supposedly to fix his electric bells for an alarm system. However, he had a large darning needle fitted to a piece of wood in his pocket, and became quite irate when I said this wasn't to be stuck in anyone. He has periods when he can be really aggravating, i.e. poking, pinching, etc. and on immediate retaliation or a 'short' remark, disappears in a sulky mood screaming abuse. On Monday evening, became very angry when a maths trick wouldn't work out but gentle encouragement to keep trying settled his immediate reaction to sulk. Once Mr A. arrived and showed him the trick again, he immediately became peacock proud, 'See Miss, I was right – you just couldn't do it!' Wednesday evening very quietly worked by his bed, making a model of a racing car (Elizabeth, blind CSV, did the final tucking in).

Very aggressive. Rude all day and evening. Physically biting, twisting my arm but at bedtime extremely gentle, insisting on hot-water bottle, sweets and tucking in. Monday evening talked a good deal about kissing him good-night, that his mum always kissed him good-night [coming from 'a very institutionalized, emotionally deprived, unintegrated boy' this was of course pure fantasy] and he didn't need anyone else. Frequently this week William has deliberately come and refused to do something, e.g. 'Quarterly Medical,

I'm not having one.' When told quite firmly and loudly, 'No more nonsense, you know perfectly well that you will have your medical', he went away quite happily. Monday night, after wire-cutting incident, was almost in tears in bed, grateful for darkness and gentleness of rubbing his forehead. This week has fluctuated between the wide angles of aggression – verbal and physical – and primary dependence.

Outwardly has become very aggressive and rude. He is still extremely aggravating towards the other boys. His main interest is birds' nesting and he delights in showing eggs to me or blowing them in my presence, especially when I've told him that I strongly disapprove. William makes comments such as 'Here's a leg'. Generally, however, he has come to rely on bedtimes as an important period. He has taken to wearing his jumper in bed and enjoys a 'game' of me taking it off, so that he is very much a baby – a two year old. The most amusing incident occurred when I used the sleeve of his pullover as a speaking tube. William enjoys his forehead being rubbed and asks for a proper goodnight kiss. He showed considerable consideration at the weekend when his socks were covered in sewage and he insisted on washing them before I did. However, William still has a sadistic streak. In his possession are several sharp instruments – a nail dart and a stick dart, locked firmly in his wardrobe. This week he hit Arthur Smithson with a chain after 10 p.m. giving Artie a black eye. I spoke to him quietly at bedtime about injuries and blindness; despite his couldn't-care-less attitude he really seemed to take the comments seriously. William too comes out at washing-up time to talk or show me what he can do. One evening he had wet socks and spent the time making patterns on the tiled floor.

His favourite saying has become 'Not really, Miss . . .' which seems to be a fair summary of himself. Our contact has been through the building of a boat, making sails and sewing on badges; unfortunately the boat sank. Not daunted, William next asked for a fishing net to be made. When later we couldn't find the material I'd given him he said sharply, 'You've taken back something you've given me.' Eventually the material was found and William let me make the net during my lunch break. He came into my flat and sat on the floor while I was sewing. He was most concerned that my coffee was getting cold. The net was a success and he has spent ages in the pool fishing for tiddlers and tadpoles. At bedtime William now accepts the fact that he is the last boy visited and waits patiently.

 . . . The same evening he told me at bedtime he wanted to see padre as he was going to run away with Ted and Harold during the night. The three left the house at 6.45 a.m. William eventually returned to David's at 10.20 p.m., brought by Mr B. Fortunately we had filled his hot-water bottle and put out his clean clothes in case he returned. William was very quiet and said that he had not had anything to eat. I took him along to my flat and cooked him sausage and chips; he talked fairly freely. William said he had been to Gloucester after giving the police the slip in Cirencester. He had caught a train to London and on the way had stuck a stick out of the window and knocked coal from another train. He then caught another train to Gloucester and walked back to the Community. Other pieces of information came such as the lift he had to Gloucester, about twelve miles by car. Every time anyone had asked him a direct question regarding, e.g. food or damp clothes he had refused help, then he added quietly, 'not really though'. When he was finally tucked in at 11.30 p.m., he was pleased with his bottle and the two sweets left under the pillow. He gave me a big hug and a kiss before settling down for the night.

A tremendous improvement in his relationships with E. and myself. William has been far more relaxed and will come and talk with me, both in the flat and in the housemother's room. The first real contact was at Whitsun when I cooked lunch for everyone. William helped a good deal, fetching and carrying, having a key to the housemother's room to fetch items. He enjoyed telling Mr C. that the preparations were all a surprise and that he knew of them. At lunch William appeared very smartly dressed, however he had forgotten to do his hair and used my bathroom to finish his toilet. During lunch William was at the centre of conversations, he was thrilled to be chosen as a reserve for the archery team going out in the afternoon. He left us all in a very cheerful mood.

I did not read the documents from which these notes were taken in any detail until I was reaching the end of my task. So beautifully do they illustrate point after point that I have tried to make about the way the Community goes to work that I was tempted to start again using these notes as a basis. Pat Drew may well be dissatisfied with the *quantity* of feminine help available at the Cotswold, but the *quality* unconsciously revealed in these notes is surely something she must rejoice in. Here was an unfeeling, vicious, 'almost sadistic' boy who could calmly flick another across the eyes with a chain. Here is the sort of boy who, if left to the influences that were hitherto open to him – if indeed subjected to the normal processes that are still current in at least some correctional establishments – would unquestionably have developed into one of those youths we read of in the newspapers, and whom we think of as being particularly odious and repugnant. Youths apparently utterly devoid of compassion or any warm feeling for others, entirely without human sympathy, who can attack another with a bicycle chain or put in the steel-shod boot without the slightest qualm. In these notes the lid has been lifted slightly and we have been able to look beneath the surface. Beneath that hard and unfeeling exterior we have seen a sad, unhappy, eager, pathetic child. I leave it to the reader to decide whether that child is best treated by means of 'discipline' and 'training', or by the kind of tender understanding, the provision of early needs, by all the things these notes reveal.

I have no idea what became of either of these boys, though I get the feeling that they both left the Community rather earlier than one might have wished. But if our criterion of success is a therapeutic and not a legalistic one, there is no doubt in my mind that we can put against their names the comment 'much helped'. Much helped not only by what they received from these two women, but also by what they received from other people, other influences, to which their efforts made the boys accessible.*

* One of the difficulties one has to face in writing about something that is continuously developing and changing is that by the time one's impressions are on paper things have developed further and what one has written is no longer true. In general I have been content to allow my account to remain as it was when I wrote it, but here I must make an exception. When I wrote this chapter things were as I described them. But the forward movement I saw and recorded in the role of women has continued so that they are no longer a separate task force working under the direction of Pat Drew. They are now well enough accepted, and their function sufficiently understood, for them to be integrated as part of the general group-living staff, under the overall direction, with their male colleagues, of the head of group living.

# 8 Towards a Single Culture

The subculture which had grown up at the Cotswold School was not peculiar to that establishment but is fairly common in some degree to penal establishments of all kinds. Indeed it is probably true to say that in all establishments in which there is a 'we' and 'they' element – staff and patients, adults and children, teachers and pupils, officers and other ranks, employers and employees – there is a tendency for each side to develop its own culture, its own mores, its own defences against the other, which is thought of as being, in however mild a sense, the enemy. The two cultures are not necessarily antipathetic in content and structure and not entirely in outlook; we have seen how the boys' culture at the Cotswold School was a kind of parody of the adult system of control and management. In establishments where one side has the duty or assumes the right of governing the other, the ruling side may often find it expedient, or even necessary, to use directly or obliquely various aspects of the culture of the ruled – to defer to some of their assumptions, to accept and to treat individuals they regard as leaders, and so on. This was a well-known feature of British Colonial administration, and like all else in love and war it may be perfectly fair and may lead to a manageable and fruitful relationship in many ordinary circumstances of life. But in a penal establishment (and I am using this old-fashioned and undesirable phrase in order to embrace all and any kind of residential establishment for those who have broken the law) an important consideration arises which makes highly undesirable such collusive acceptance of the residents' culture by the 'rulers' – the staff – as it is likely to defeat the ends for which the establishment exists. That consideration is simply that the inmate subculture of a penal institution is based on the very mores – the delinquent mores – from which it is a function of the establishment to wean its inmates. The fact that in structure and content it seems to parody the formal institution culture must not blind us to the fact that in motivation and in its goals it is anti-social and delinquent, and any collusion with it must be fatal to the primary purpose of the staff. We may be forgiven if we sometimes wonder whether the structure and sanctions of the formal culture do not derive from those of the subculture instead of the reverse. Let us look at an American institution for adolescents.

In his *Cottage Six* Howard Polsky is concerned to show how, in the institution of which he was writing, the inmate culture was so strong and influential, pervading as it did the whole of the lives of the inmates for twenty-four hours every day, that it had a greater effect upon the boys than did the specific therapeutic measures introduced by the professional staff, which are seen almost as merely incidental. The author makes various suggestions for remedying this state of affairs – that the 'professional staff' (in his context counsellors, social workers, psychotherapists) should be somehow integrated into the residential life of the establishment instead of being isolated in consulting rooms on a nine-to-five basis; that the child-care staff should be upgraded and trained in the skills of environment therapy; and that the staff should seek to penetrate and influence the inmate culture. I mention this book only to show how successfully the Cotswold Community avoided the various pitfalls to which Polsky refers. In the first place they have never distinguished between 'professional' and 'child-care' staff. To them, from the beginning, child-care staff have been regarded as professional people who are the very backbone of the environment therapy which is the purpose of the Community. This is not to say that everyone who joins the child-care staff arrives a highly skilled and trained environmental therapist; but it is realized that the total day-to-day living experience is what is going to influence the residents, and staff are trained, helped and encouraged to see their fundamental role in making that experience rich and positive and fruitful – in fact therapeutic. They have not sought to 'penetrate the inmate culture' but have gone about achieving the same end by an entirely different means. The existing inmate culture was to all intents and purposes destroyed, partly by breaking up the institution into small and more autonomous groups, and partly by the abandonment of the hierarchical structure. The power-and-violence basis of the inmate culture reflected the formal power-and-punishment structure of the staff; that structure being no longer there it cannot be reflected, and in so far as the inmates create a new subculture reflecting the existing staff structure (if indeed they do) it cannot be so harmful in its effect as the old parody was. But the hope is that the need to elaborate a specific inmate culture will be much diminished by the fact that the absence of the power-and-punishment complex and its replacement by genuine personal authority based on real concern means that – while there may always be a division between adults and children – the adults are not regarded as 'natural enemies' to the same degree that they are in orthodox autocratic institutions. The hope is that there will grow up, not an inmate culture to be penetrated and influenced (or destroyed) by the staff, but a genuine community culture which permeates and motivates the whole place, which is influenced by and which influences all who live there, boys and staff alike. It is integral to the concept of this kind of group culture that its form, structure and content cannot be foreseen because it grows from the living experience of the group, and from the lesser groups within the total group; and its image will (if it is true to its vital purpose) change and vary from time to time. Its basis is the belief that a true group experience (as distinct from a gang-and-boss-clique experience) is enriching to the individuals who constitute it. The only way in which it is managed or manipulated is that the principal ensures that he filters into it a sufficient number of stable people (the staff) committed to the conviction that it must remain a genuine group experience and never become a power-dominated gang culture.

Howard Jones, in his *Reluctant Rebels*, draws a very clear picture of the two communities that invariably grow up in the normal authoritarian institution, and how these communities have not only different cultures but also different and often mutually opposed aims. For example a common situation is where one of the two 'communities' – the staff – is vested with all power and all authority, and is concerned with making rules, often tedious or oppressive, for the governing of the others; while the other community, with no formal power and no responsibility, works hard at finding means of circumventing those rules. He suggests – to my mind convincingly – that in establishments where the staff have been able to share some of their responsibilities and power with the inmates, there has been a tendency for the two 'communities' to coalesce; and that the degree of this coalescence is the degree to which the power group have been willing to share with the inmate group. This is surely very much the same sort of thing as the 'one culture' towards which the Cotswold Community strives, and is an important aspect of the concept of shared responsibility. We have seen how Balbernie refused from the start to be the 'omnipotent god' of the Community, but it is important to remember that staff cannot be expected to share responsibilities until they have some responsibilities to share! So there has been a constant pushing of responsibility downwards, though this very expression is out of context because it implicitly affirms the hierarchy which the Cotswold is concerned to deny. It is based on the existing assumption of most of us that responsibility and power are 'at the top'. It is the kind of assumption made by new staff, and it is certainly the kind of assumption made by the boys. It is an assumption that is gradually beginning to give way, at the Cotswold, to an acceptance of the idea that a number of people living together all have a measure of responsibility for each other. This is crucial, it is fundamental to the whole treatment process as it concerns delinquent young people – the replacement of a crude, individualistic, blind self-seeking, of the kind that motivates the power-violence subculture, by concern and consideration for others. We saw earlier how the staff in each cottage unit were required to assume basic responsibility for the boys in their unit, sharing that responsibility with colleagues within the Community – teaching staff, head of group living, therapeutic consultant – and with others outside the Community – parents, social workers and so on. Thus responsibility for the care and treatment of the boys and the general conduct of the establishment as a whole is widely diffused throughout and among the people in contact with the boys, instead of being forever channelled along a line of command from the top of a pyramidal structure. The next step, which the Community is now tentatively taking, is to diffuse the responsibility still further and wider – among the boys. It will be up to the staff of each unit to go about this in the way that seems to them – to use an old Quaker phrase – to 'speak to the condition' of the boys in their particular group. This will not come quickly or easily because most of us – and especially those of us who are drawn to the traditional power-exercising jobs like teaching, the prison service, child care or even social work – are often unconsciously motivated against anything that seems to detract from the personal imposing of our will upon others. But whatever our unconscious motivation, the idea of people 'in authority' consulting, suggesting, asking, instead of simply *telling* the inmates, is quite outside our customary experience, and we tend to feel such an approach to be a threat to our own authority and security.

So a great deal of learning has to take place among the staff, and it has to be largely learning from experience; the experience of sharing responsibility and talking things out with colleagues in the first place, and later, experimentally, with the boys. It has to be learning *by* staff, not teaching *of* staff, because, as Balbernie said to me, this is something that has to be caught, not taught – though I suspect nevertheless that there is a good deal of that admirable kind of teaching that consists merely of the communication of an enthusiasm.

As their stature grows, and their confidence increases, adults more and more discuss things with boys, consult with them, seek their opinion on the small matters of everyday concern. I heard them in the Cottage one day asking what the boys thought of the idea of having tea in the Cottage in future instead of going over to the dining hall for it. These were the least integrated boys in the Community who are not thought of as being yet able to be 'other-regarding' or to accept real responsibility. They saw immediately what was in it for *them* (it was much cosier and pleasanter to eat at home) but the problems involved – the fetching of food, keeping it warm, or alternatively cooking it, the washing up afterwards – all had to be explained to them. This was clearly an educational experience for these so far hardly educable boys. They could not of course – these particular boys – be expected to elaborate and maintain a system for permanently coping with these problems, though in their eagerness to achieve the end they cheerfully expressed willingness to look after the means; but other boys, more integrated boys in other units, certainly could, and do. I was told for example of the boys in the newly established Orchard unit. No system had yet been organized for getting the supper dishes washed, volunteers would be sought and often not found, so that the adults did far more than their fair share of this chore. One day, quite spontaneously I gather, a boy said, 'Why don't we get this dishwashing organized?' – and a rota system was quickly arranged. A small thing but, in my view, an important one. It would have been perfectly simple for the staff to make and impose such a rota and it would have been, perhaps grudgingly, accepted. It would have been accepted, however, not as a means of solving a social problem (for such in its small way this was), but as something the staff wanted done. The arrangement that was actually made was one that involved first the acceptance of a responsibility, and second the sharing of it. It was the beginning of social concern, it was even one aspect of the beginning of the Cotswold culture based on social awareness, on the caring of each for all, instead of on self-assertion, glorification of violence and the weakest to the wall.

This is only a beginning and no one at the Cotswold Community would see it as anything else. Such small beginnings moreover are appearing here and there in all manner of ways and places.

No one who has not enjoyed the experience of habitually consulting with children, instead of merely telling them, can know how difficult it is to *begin*, and for most of the people coming to the Cotswold this was a beginning. It was thought therefore that staff might be helped if some small structure were to be erected in the form of a 'pocket' of time each day devoted to the purpose of adult–child consultation – a meeting together of all who constituted a living unit. In every unit therefore from nine to nine-thirty each morning a meeting of the group takes place, to discuss any subject that anyone wants to raise. The time and the opportunity are provided; what emerges will depend upon what each particular group is able to make of it. In general discussions are not structured, there is no imposition of the formal ritual of agenda and officers. The purpose is not so much to reach a decision, much less to 'pass a resolution' (though there is no reason why a group should not do that if it is so disposed), as to throw light on something that is worrying somebody. The meeting does of course provide an opportunity for the unit leader to make necessary announcements, but its real purpose is to discuss, and if possible solve, any problem that has arisen, to seek to understand any recent untoward happening, perhaps to air and settle grievances, certainly to make plans for future activities and projects, even if it is only to decide what TV programme to watch that evening.

It may well be that in the early stages some anxious adults will tend to think of the meeting as a concession conferred by them upon children, and any who approach it in that way will try to keep things very much in their own hands, acting as a 'strong' chairman, narrowly limiting the subjects to be discussed, forbidding certain kinds of comment. As they become more accustomed to this kind of discussion their anxieties will diminish, their confidence increase, and as they become more relaxed, so will the discussions. Not only more relaxed, but freer, more wide-ranging and more relevant to needs. Then will the adults begin to apprehend in reality (if hitherto their acceptance of this fact has been a theoretical one) that the group discussions are not merely across adult–child frontiers, but across other frontiers too; that the meeting is not of two groups, one senior, trying to 'help' the other, but a many-faceted agglomeration of personalities all able at various times to contribute to each other's needs; that the group of people who assemble every morning are 'gelling' into a real group which is developing its own dynamic, its own ethos, its own *culture*; that the group can contribute to adult needs as well as to those of children. It is also an unhappy fact that if a group leader's anxieties do not diminish sufficiently for him to allow a group ethos to develop – if he insists on maintaining a tight dominating control – then he is probably working at the wrong job.

Fortunately the group leader who is learning in this way does not have to learn in a vacuum, entirely unaided. He has ample opportunity for discussing what is going on in his group with colleagues, including of course the head of group living, and he

can, if he so wishes, seek help in interpreting his group's behaviour, at the weekly session with the therapeutic consultant.

The morning meetings then are one of the means by which
the Cotswold Community works towards – and through which
it expresses – a common culture, but of course they do many
more specific things in the process. One of the major problems
of any work with delinquents is that of communication. Therapeutic work cannot be carried out – indeed no work can be
carried out – unless there is good two-way communication
between those involved in it. Difficulty of communication is one
of the symptoms of emotional disorder. The emotionally distressed person does communicate, and often very dramatically,
but so often his communication is by what one might describe
as a 'deed-code' – by acting out. The skilled and perceptive
worker can often interpret this code, but if he always has to
rely on that kind of communication he may often be too late.
The acting out may consist of running away, and no great harm
may come of that. But the running away could also involve
car theft, and a car inexpertly driven by a distressed teenager
can be deadly. So one of the virtues of meetings is that they
encourage and facilitate verbal communication. This does not
mean that a disturbed adolescent learns thereby to give precise
verbal articulation to his inner tensions. What he does learn
is to *talk* in code instead of *acting* in code. The more he talks
the more he reveals, though the subject under discussion may
have no outward relation at all to the inner stress he is communicating. To take the first hypothetical example that springs
to mind; pathological sibling jealousy is often to be found
among disturbed and delinquent young people, and in a residential setting they are apt to displace that jealousy upon a
member of the group with which they live. At meetings and
discussions such feelings are often expressed in bitter and quite
irrational opposition to everything that is said by the subject
of this jealousy. Where there are no such discussions the boy
will have recourse instead to petty persecution or even harsh
and tyrannical bullying. He may well indeed attempt this in
addition to the verbal expression, but if he does it will be less
violent because the verbal outlet has in some measure abated
the need; and in any case his victim has access to redress by

bringing up such attacks at the meeting. If the victim feels unable to raise the matter (as well he may) someone else can, and in the ensuing discussion the aggressor may well begin to learn at least a little about what really motivates his persecution. But whether his verbal persecution or in the discussion of his physical violence, he is all the time saying things, however oblique, however expressed, that are helping his environing adults to know and to understand him better. It is not likely that he will learn in group discussion a great deal about his unconscious motivation, but he will learn that his conduct is unacceptable not only to his victim, not only to adults, but also to his peers, and he is thus motivated to greater efforts to keep it in check. For this is another purpose of group discussion – to enable its participants to learn that certain minimum standards of conduct are not something that are required of us by remotely imposed law, or by adults (who are commonly assumed by adolescents to be unsympathetic), but even by their own age group and social class, even by those of their peers who are least able in their own lives to sustain such standards.

Improved communications; the recognition of standards; these are two of the major advantages deriving from group meetings. There are many others of which I will mention only one – the educational value and the general enhancement of personality that comes from accepting a measure of responsibility for and sharing in, the planning of group routines and group activities. This is learning by doing in a very real sense, and there are surely few who will attempt to deny that the active participant in a truly democratic society is a bigger, richer, more aware person than one who merely accepts what is handed down from some remote government or superior, whether benign or malign. In a democratic society such as ours aspires to be this does not need to be argued.

One other thing needs to be reiterated. The Cotswold Community does not see this single culture developing according to any preconceived pattern. They see it as part of the general pattern of human relationships at the Community, relationships characterized, so far as the adults are concerned, by concern, by tolerance, by a relaxed and egalitarian absence of pomp and false dignity, by sympathetic understanding of each other's difficulties, by a total, non-collusive non-acceptance of delinquent behaviour coupled with a total and loving acceptance of the person guilty of it. An important aspect too is that understanding and respectful recognition by each sex of the specific role and contribution of the other, of which I spoke at some length in the previous chapter. All these qualities and attitudes will, it is hoped, through free communication 'rub off' in some measure on the boys or be ingested by them through the process of identification. But the people in each unit are different from the people in every other unit, so while a common Cotswold culture will come into being, its precise manifestation will vary, its colouring will be different from unit to unit, and each unit will experiment with and develop and vary its own form of expression of that culture, its own internal machinery. The Cotswold Community is a living organism that is growing; it is not a structure that is being put together from an architect's drawing. For this reason its ultimate form cannot be predicted, and if it ever achieves an 'ultimate form' its usefulness will be ended.

# 9 'The Modality being Love'

I started this book with what some will consider to be an attack
on approved schools. Let me therefore in this final chapter say
something in their defence; or if not in their defence, at least in
mitigation. It is something that must never be forgotten by
those who – like myself – are apt to be critical of approved
schools. It is something of which Richard Balbernie reminded
me almost every time I visited the Cotswold Community, so I
could hardly forget it even if I were otherwise likely to do so.
The approved schools had to take what they were sent, and
what they were sent included in the nature of things the failed
residue of all the other services for dealing with disturbed,
maladjusted, unstable and delinquent children. When parents,
teachers, parsons and youth workers had done what they could;
when the second line of defence – the child-guidance service,
the schools for maladjusted children, the child-care service – had
done its best and failed; when the courts had tried the condi-
tional discharge, the supervision order, the probation order,
fines, attendance centres – when all these as well as the fit-
person order had been tried, and failed, then the child was
committed to an approved school. I do not mean that no child
ever reached an approved school without having first been
subjected to all these remedial and punitive efforts, but few
reached a school without one or some of these expedients having
first been tried, and *some* had been through almost everything.
Among this failed residue were some with whom, if we are to
be quite honest, we must confess that society simply does not
know how to deal. They may be psychopathic personalities or
affectionless children or frozen children or what you will, and
certainly some of them will be in the early stages of a psychotic
disorder. After all the sieving and sorting and screening, what
came through the final net went to the approved school. And
they – the schools – could not say 'This child or that child is
not suitable for approved-school training.' The court in its

wisdom had committed them, and the approved school had to take them. Only if, after admission, a psychiatrist thought they ought to be in a mental hospital could the approved school escape its responsibility. Even schools staffed by the most highly trained, skilled and devoted people could not hope to succeed with every one of those of whom society had despaired, and the best that could be expected in some cases was that the schools would keep them out of circulation for a year or two. The approved-school order is now a thing of the past, and approved schools have begun the process by which they become part of the general child-care service of the local authorities. But whatever we choose to call residential establishments for children in the future, and however we organize our methods of trying to help children who find it difficult to fit in with the expectations of society, these residual cases will still be with us; these are indeed and very literally the 'dangerous and perishing classes'.

I am not among those who regard such young people as utterly irreclaimable; the trouble is that the subtle, patient and learned skills that are necessary to treat them successfully are as yet not nearly widespread enough for us to be able to deal at present with more than a tiny fraction of them. For the rest, for some years yet, the best we shall be able to offer will still be the holding operation that has hitherto been carried out – and carried out somewhat thanklessly because these were called the failures of the system – by the approved schools. I believe a place like the Cotswold Community would be able to deal constructively with a small number of these residual children, but even if such a place were to deal with them and them alone it would touch only the fringe of the problem. But the probability is – and our absolute knowledge of how to deal with deeply disturbed and delinquent children is as yet so scanty that we can only talk about probabilities – the probability is that it would be a mistake to fill a community home entirely with these hard core residuals.

What they are trying to do at the Cotswold is to work in the area of the 'probabilities' in the hope of finding one or two or, if they are very successful, more than one or two points at which it may become possible to say 'highly probable' instead of merely probable. They do not know the answers, and few things infuriate them more than the assumption that they think they do. They are merely looking for the answers and they are bringing to bear on the search learning, skill, patience and professional competence to such a degree that they cannot fail to find some answers to some questions. They are not setting up a model, as some people have tended to assume, for all community homes to copy. Community homes will be dealing with a variety of children that is almost infinite in its diversity. To suggest that there is a single 'model' way of dealing with them all would be ludicrous, and none know that better than those at the Cotswold Community. They have been anxious to impress upon me all along that judgements as to whether their work is 'better' than the earlier work are futile because like can only be compared with like, and they see their task as intrinsically different from the task of the approved school. In this I think they are bending over backwards to be kind to approved schools, but certainly one vital difference is that they do not feel themselves obliged as the approved schools were to take all comers, with some of whom they would be able to do little more than merely hold them for a time and perhaps prevent deterioration. They reject this not because they see it as no longer necessary, as I have just suggested, it is going to be necessary for a long time yet; but because they believe no establishment can do everything, and they have set themselves the task of trying to give positive constructive help to boys in respect of whom there seems to be some hope that they might respond to the therapeutic influences which the Community generates. This does not mean that they confine themselves to the 'easy' cases. This is the jibe (for that is what it is) that is always used by the ignorant, against those establishments which are skilled enough and professional enough to use sophisticated selection techniques and criteria. On the contrary, the task they have set themselves at the Cotswold is that of trying to find and to operate ways of helping those whose delinquency is due to deep emotional disturbance. They are beginning to realize that this kind of causation is much more common than they once thought; and of course it is a class which includes some of those hardcore residuals of which I have just been speaking. There are for example the unintegrated boys at whom we looked briefly earlier, and one of the things that has become clear is that one such boy can totally disrupt – can hardly avoid totally disrupting – any small group in which he is placed. At the Cotswold therefore these boys live together in one living unit with specially trained, concerned people looking after them, and are introduced gradually to other groups as they become more integrated and hence less disruptive. They do not assert that there is no longer a place for the establishment that is run on traditional, authoritarian lines; so far as they can see there may well be a continuous need for such places among the variety of methods and techniques which will, it is hoped, be deployed within the system of community homes. But they believe that for the type of boy with whom *they* are concerned, something different is called for.

They are far from asserting that they know exactly what that different something is with any exactitude – that they know how to convert these unhappy troubled youngsters into stable and purposeful adults. They are an experimental institution, they are seeking the answers. I happen to believe that the area in which they are carrying out their search – the area of human feeling and interpersonal reactions and relationships – is a very fruitful one and I am sure they will find *some* answers. But if and when some answers have been found, they will not constitute a final solution, nor a specific model for all other community homes. Community homes will have to specialize, and the regime and methods of any specific home will depend upon the kind of child with whom it deals. The Cotswold Community does not presume to tell any of them how to go about their job, but it is none the less my conviction that many of them will be able to learn something from what is now being done at the Cotswold. I am sure that it is out of the kind of feeling about people, the kind of concern for them that I have tried to convey in these pages, that all efforts to help the offender must grow. There is still – in my view – a long way to go before that approach is as universal as it must become, and until then the offender will remain as so often he is today, the victim of the need we all feel for a scapegoat.

It is easy to criticize the Cotswold in all kinds of ways, but no one criticizes it more harshly than do the people who are doing the work; and this self-criticism is not just sporadic and incidental – it is deliberate and organized. Every month each of the four senior workers writes a long and detailed report of that department of the work for which he is responsible while the principal writes another. These are not so much a report of the work as a critique of it, and while each speaks from the point of view of his own particular responsibilities, his comments, because he speaks as one of a team, are not necessarily restricted to his own work, but may refer to the work as a whole. By this means the whole project is under constant, continuous critical appraisal. I have read these documents and they are as far removed as can be imagined from the kind of complacent, self-laudatory 'report' that often goes to school managers or subscribers; and they go, *in toto*, to the Home Office, to the County Council and to the Inspector. These reports examine not only the way in which various ideas and methods are being put into practice, and how far, if at all, they are meeting with success, and if not why not; they quite often question the validity of concepts which earlier they had been inclined to accept, not because they have airily 'changed their minds', but on the basis of their continued assessment of the value of those concepts in day-to-day use. 'This rage was right i' the main,' you hear them saying with Browning, 'that acquiescence vain.' This is the way in which they seek those 'answers', with sharp self-appraisal and great integrity of purpose.

Quite apart from this organized and ongoing criticism, talk, discussion and argument goes on the whole time. Even the most committed of the workers can see faults and failings, which they are not eager to discuss with outsiders in case they should be construed as evidence of disloyalty. I did hear one or two of these questionings to which there seemed to me to be perfectly good answers – I did not give the answers then because it was not my function to instruct the staff.

I talked to, or more precisely was talked to by, a man who had been at the Cotswold School for some years and was now an enthusiastic member of the staff of the Cotswold Community. 'Mind *you*,' he said (or words to this effect), 'there's one thing that seems a bit strange. In the old days when we had about

120 boys, there were only two members of the staff who didn't actually work, as you might say, at the coalface, in actual daily contact with the boys, as teachers, instructors and housemasters. They were the head and his deputy. Now, with about half the number of boys, you have the principal, the head of group living (who doesn't run a house himself), the head of education (who doesn't take a class), the bursar, the social-case worker, none of whom work a seam, have daily duties with a group of boys.' The facts are indeed as my friend stated them; but the comparison he attempted to draw was totally invalid. He over-looked the very point I have just been making, that the School and the Community were not doing the same job. Talk, discussion, comparing of notes, exchange of information are all basic to the idea of the therapeutic community, and are going on continually all the time. Unless they do the community will fail of its therapeutic purpose. All this talk, this dissemination of information, of views as well as of facts, is not aimless and undirected; it is constructive, purposeful and organized. It needs, if it is to be both dynamic and fruitful, people whose job it is to act as catalysts, people who will see that the fermentation is continuous, and that everyone is both a contributor to and a beneficiary of this fertilizing stream of words. Those people who are accused of not hewing at the coalface are continually attending meetings of one kind or another of different groups of people for one purpose or another, and such meetings and discussions are part of the life-blood of a therapeutic community.

But that is not all. What they are trying to do at the Cotswold Community is, it is true, to set up a therapeutic community, but they are attempting to do more than that. They are – as we saw just now – trying to keep their operation under continuous self-examination and they are doing that because they see themselves as an experimental institution treading new paths which they attempt to chart as they tread them. This is another reason why they are not to be thought of as a 'model' – not all community homes will need to be so agonizingly and voluminously self-critical; and it is another reason why there is so relatively large a number of adults who are not in regular daily contact with groups of boys. Even that is not all. The work of the Community is work in which up to now very few people are trained, skilled and experienced. The staff have to learn as they go along, and the people whose job it is to make sure that that learning is taking place, and taking place along the right lines, are those same senior people. They are certainly not an example of Parkinson's Law.

Another criticism I succeeded in evoking, though not without a certain amount of provocative prodding of the junior staff, was this: the Cotswold Community professes to have done away with the hierarchical staff structure but, I am told, there are still several people around who seem to have a good deal of power and authority. This remark both misconceives what is meant by eradicating the hierarchical structure, and at the same time demonstrates how successful they have been in doing so. In the hierarchical structure the person at the top has all power, all authority, all knowledge and all wisdom. Only he can take any decision of any importance, and even those decisions he does not personally make are made in his name. Only he possesses the necessary knowledge to make decisions because information tends to pass up and down from the base perimeter of the cone or pyramid, to the apex where the head man sits. Only through him, generally speaking, is there any meaningful contact with the outside world so far as it affects boys living in the place. Dispensing with this kind of structure does not mean, as these young people seemed to think, that henceforward nobody has any authority to make decisions or power to see that they are implemented. On the contrary, it means that more people have that power and that authority, each in his own sphere. I suspect that the young critics were thinking chiefly of the head of group living and the head of education, each of whom, in crude terminology, is boss in his own sphere. But each of these men is striving – and striving it seemed to me with a good deal of success – to encourage his colleagues to accept responsibility, to exercise authority, to make decisions and initiate projects, and this is all part of the learning process to which I have just referred. I had the interesting experience of eavesdropping one day on an urgent, hurried discussion behind the kitchen door in the Cottage. There were present five people – the housemother, the deputy housefather (it was the housefather's day off), a member of the teaching staff who had 'secondary duties' in the Cottage, a CSV girl acting as deputy housemother, and another person whose function I do not recall. The problem was something like this: an exceptionally difficult, disturbed boy – such as all in the Cottage were – had recently gone out and committed some delinquency which had come to the notice of the police. It was not in itself a very serious affair but the police were apparently proposing to reactivate a previous charge which it was thought they had dropped, and the two charges together might seem to the bench so serious as to warrant drastic action. The boy did not yet know this but was already alarmed enough. The questions under discussion were, should they warn the boy *now* that there was danger of the earlier offence coming up and thus prepare him for it, or should they first try a little more persuasion with the police? Should they reassure him about their willingness to keep him at the Community when this might be interpreted by the boy as pre-empting the decision of the court? In urgent whispers behind the kitchen door just as it was time to go to work, policies were determined, decisions made.

'I can't stop, I've got eight boys waiting for me, but I'm concerned about this boy, and my view is . . .'

'We mustn't be long – he's in the sitting-room now expecting someone to come and talk to him. Shall we . . .'

'Ought we to. . . . Perhaps we should . . .'

'Shall we get in touch with the parents, or shall we wait a bit and see what action the police are really going to take? Perhaps they won't prosecute after all if someone talks to them.'

'We should scatter – it looks very conspiratorial whispering behind the door like this. . . .'

I have not recorded all the discussion, but there is enough here, it seems to me, to show the new structure at work. Here were the people who were actually concerned with the boy making the necessary decisions about him, decisions which in many a more orthodox establishment could only have been made by the head. But no one said 'Ring the office and see what we are to do.' No one said, 'Will the principal agree to his staying here after this offence if the court allows it?' The decisions were theirs. One of *them* would talk to the police, not some superior officer (unless they felt that the police would be more responsive to someone with a resounding title, in which case they would ask some such person to speak to the police). If parents were to be consulted, one of *them* would do the consulting. The responsibility was theirs, the authority was theirs and they acted accordingly.

This was an example, it seems to me, of the acceptance of responsibility and the taking of vital decisions by the actual people 'working the seam', to revert to that vivid metaphor, and I valued this episode for that reason. But I valued it even more for another. These five busy people huddled hurriedly and conspiratorially behind that kitchen door were expressing something which is the most vital, the most impressive and the most touching thing about the Cotswold Community. Those five people were all moved by the boy's distress and were expressing a deeply felt concern for his well-being. Ideas, methods, concepts, theories are all valuable and essential. But they are all useless without the genuine loving concern for the child. I have spoken of all the talk that goes on at the Cotswold, and with its sesquipedalian prolixity it is rather the talk of men than of angels, but I have a deep conviction that it is neither sounding brass nor tinkling cymbals, and I am convinced of it for the reason that Paul gave when he gave us that image; it is informed with love.

Love is not a word you will often hear at the Cotswold, but its presence is unmistakable. Neither will you hear much talk of religion because its presence is a reality and not merely a system of observances. All formal compulsory religious observance was abandoned in the early days of the Community; neither the chaplain nor the principal believed it was possible to impose in this way something that is so intensely personal, something which belongs to one's inmost being, something which, while it may have many faces and many voices, speaks only to the heart of a man when he is ready to listen. I found Richard Balbernie most reluctant to talk about his own religious life though in fact it was he who broached the subject. He did so because an account of the Cotswold Community which made no reference to the spring, the source and motive of all that goes on there would be false and misleading. He has been conscious throughout of strength other than his own without which he would not have been able to continue, and others have been conscious also of this strength. Certainly so far as Balbernie is concerned he is highly qualified in the technical sense for the work upon which he is engaged, but these qualifications have been sought in order that he might the more effectively give expression to his personal conviction (a conviction which is also mine) that the 'cure' for delinquency is to be found in the Gospels. Not, that is to say, in trying to make Christians, but in trying to give expression to that which lies at the core of Christian teaching.

So I am back again at that word which I said is so little heard at the Cotswold. Perhaps I may end with a quotation from a paper read by the late Derek Morrell to an audience of approved-school heads, Home Office inspectors, criminologists and psychiatrists. He was speaking of the educational role of approved schools, but his words seem to me to sum up most admirably the aim and purpose of the Cotswold Community.

And this is the purpose of education : to foster the growth of loving persons – who are aware both of their individuality and of their membership one of another, who accept one another, communicate with one another, and who (understanding their own interdependent nature) choose to use their experience creatively, in cooperation with other people. In short it is to enable people to live creatively in a creative community, harmoniously blending their own independence with the independence of others, the modality being love.

# Further Reading

These are some of the many books that have been published during the last decade which throw some light on approved schools, or contribute to an understanding of the approach now being used at the Cotswold Community.

**R. Balbernie**, *Residential Work with Children*, Pergamon, 1966.

**W. R. Bion**, *Experiences with Groups*, Tavistock, 1961.

**J. Carlebach**, *Caring for Children in Trouble*, Routledge & Kegan Paul, 1970.

**B. Dockar-Drysdale**, *Therapy in Child Care*, Longman, 1969.

**Home Office Advisory Council**, *Care and Treatment in a Planned Environment*, HMSO, 1970.

**H. Jones**, *Reluctant Rebels*, Tavistock, 1962.

**M. Jones**, *Beyond the Therapeutic Community*, Yale University Press, 1968.

**H. W. Polsky**, *Cottage Six*, Wiley, 1965.

**G. Rose**, *Schools for Young Offenders*, Tavistock, 1967.

**R. F. Sparks** and **R. G. Hood** (eds.), *The Residential Treatment of Disturbed and Delinquent Boys*, Institute of Criminology, 1968.

**W. David Wills**, *Throw Away Thy Rod*, Gollancz, 1960; *The Hawkspur Experiment*, 2nd edn, Allen & Unwin, 1967.

**D. W. Winnicott**, *The Maturational Process and the Facilitating Environment*, Hogarth Press, 1965.

Mention should also be made of two early pioneers in the field of the therapeutic approach to young offenders in a residential setting, August Aichhorn and Homer Lane.

**A. Aichhorn**, *Wayward Youth*, Putnam, 1936.

**E. T. Bazeley**, *Homer Lane and the Little Commonwealth*, Allen & Unwin, 1928.

**W. David Wills**, *Homer Lane: A Biography*, Allen & Unwin, 1964.

# Other Penguin Books

**Adolescent Boys in East London**

*Peter Willmott*

A classic study of boys growing up in Bethnal Green, by one of the authors of *Family and Kinship in East London*.

'Vividly written, this study draws on interviews as well as diaries kept by young men, though all of these are subjected to statistical controls. Essentially Willmott is describing young people *in process*; we see the homes they come from, and the schools they pass through, *en route* to the world of work and the new families they themselves will create . . . suggests some things that might be done to ease the strains of adolescence.'
Peter Worsley in the *Guardian*

'Reads so well, while yet offering facts and ideas of real value to teachers, youth leaders and social workers, that one feels it is almost unfair to the more pedestrian, journalistic offerings of other sociologists. Here one can learn more about teenage boys' attitudes to work, school, youth clubs, delinquency and many other matters of concern, and *enjoy* the learning, too.'
*The Times Educational Supplement*

'It is a model of its kind, exactly on target, impeccably collated and always very readable.'
Dennis Potter in *New Society*

**Children in Distress**

*Alec Clegg and Barbara Megson*

Two out of every hundred children have to be given direct help
by the State – whether it be psychiatric, social or medical.

But are these the only children 'in distress'? What about those
children who do not qualify for State help?

Alec Clegg and Barbara Megson estimate that perhaps 12 per cent
of our children desperately need help, but do not qualify to receive
it. *Children in distress* paints an agonizing picture of child distress,
based on the authors' long experience in educational administration.
They argue that it is the schools – in daily contact with the children
who are the agencies best suited to help this large and saddening
section of our child population.

'. . . this book, containing a wealth of information and ideas based
on the experience of very many schools, can help teachers who
want to help their problem pupils, but just do not know how to
start. It can help them, probably, more than any other single
volume.'
*The Times Educational Supplement*

A Penguin Education Special

**The Insecure Offenders**

Rebellious Youth in the Welfare State

*T. R. Fyvel*

The term 'juvenile delinquency' scarcely describes the world-wide malaise of youth which beset the 1950s and which – although Teddy Boys are now almost period pieces – continues into this decade. What causes this rebellion of youth in a Welfare State?

T. R. Fyvel's survey is in the tradition of George Orwell. He conjures up for us a world of sharp clothes, gang life, coffee-bars, motor-bikes, juke-boxes, pin-tables, cafés and cinemas, and adroitly relates the toe-tapping young non-conformers of today to the conditions of an affluent society which for them is little better than a dead end. This is incomparably the best study of a grave post-war phenomenon in Britain.

'An admirable book – balanced, humane, perceptive and thorough.' *New Statesman*

'As an account of all that it means to be out of step in contemporary society his book deserves to be widely read for its detachment and humanity.' *Economist*

**The Young Offender**

*D. J. West*

Criminal statistics are often quoted to prove that crime is increasing, above all among young people. Actually the picture is more complicated and less dismal.

In this balanced study of Dr Donald West, of the Cambridge Institute of Criminology, fully examines the extent, nature, causes and prevention of offences committed by those under twenty-one in England. Most convicted persons, he admits, are young males : but that is nothing new. It remains true that the incidence of conviction declines dramatically after the age of fourteen (which is the peak) and begins to peter out among those in their twenties. Delinquency, in short – and that means, to a large extent, theft in one form or another or very petty crime – is a passing phase of youth.

Donald West devotes his central chapters to the social, hereditary and psychological factors in delinquency and his final chapters to the penal and remedial measures at present being applied. A special chapter covers the more sensational topics of girls, sex, drugs and violence, which rate the bold type in the press but feature quite small in the statistics of crime.